BIG FRIEND, LITTLE FRIEND

Memoirs of a World War II Fighter Pilot

BIG FRIEND, LITTLE FRIEND

Memoirs of a World War II Fighter Pilot

RICHARD E. TURNER
Lt. Col. USAF, Ret.

Illustrations by the Author

CHAMPLIN FIGHTER MUSEUM PRESS, MESA, ARIZONA

Library of Congress Cataloging in Publication Data

Turner, Richard E.
Big Friend, little friend.

Includes index.
1. Turner, Richard E. 2. Fighter pilots—United States—Biography. 3. World War, 1939-1945—aerial operations, American. 4. United States. Army Air Forces. Fighter Group, 354th—History. 5. Korean War, 1950-1953—Aerial operations, American. I. Title.

UG626.2.T87A33 1983 940.54'4973 83-70732
ISBN 0912173009

Cover Illustration by Bob Stevens

Printed in the United States of America

THIS BOOK is dedicated to those fighter pilots known and unknown who have left and will leave in the future something of themselves in the interest of brotherly concern for their brothers in arms in the vast skies above enemy territory, far beyond the reach of friendly aid or succor.

INDIVIDUAL DEDICATION is made to James H. Howard, Brigadier General, M.O.H., who in the author's opinion epitomizes all those selfless qualities of courage, skill, and determination which as an outstanding combat leader of World War II Fighter Pilots he freely instilled in others by constant demonstration in action.

LIST OF ILLUSTRATIONS

18. Captain Jack Bradley, CO of the 353rd Squadron.

19. Captain Bob Stephens, CO of the 355th Squadron.

20. Bob Stephens' plane, *Killer*.

21. Aces in a huddle.

22. Jim Howard's P-51B "*Ding Hao*."

23. The P-51B used to fly General Eisenhower on personal combat reconnaissance.

24. and 25. Saint Lo, France, before and after the breakthrough.

26. Author escorting "Big Friends."

27. General Weyland presents Cluster to the Presidential Citation of the 354th Group.

28. My last Mustang.

29. "Turk" Teschner.

30. The end of a FW-190.

31. Mini-reunion.

32. In Korea.

356TH FIGHTER SQUADRON

354TH FIGHTER GROUP

CHAPTER 1

Like a great many youngsters in the fall of 1941 I was busily engaged in college preparing myself for what I thought was to be a useful civilian course in the years ahead. I was aware of the aggressive unfolding of the new Nazi ideology which appeared to be bent on devouring the whole of Europe through fear and force. Even though this violent upheaval outraged and disturbed me, the insulation of its remoteness and my immediate problems as a student belied any suspicion that these foreign events would change the expected path of my life. Consequently, the shocking reality of the December 7, 1941, attack on Pearl Harbor proved to be the cataclysmic catalyst effecting this change.

With the onslaught of war my mind was shorn of its preoccupation with the normal pursuits of college life, and I began to mull and explore how I might participate in the conflict ahead. As most people of twenty-one years I was strong in ideals, but weak in experience. However, of one thing I was sure: It was the aerial battle that I wanted to be a part of and I was determined to volunteer if possible in this branch of service. As a young sprout I had been an avid consumer of all tales and stories, fact or fiction, concerning the adventures of that swashbuckling gallant band of warriors who cut their niche in history fighting resolutely in the skies through World War I as fighter pilots. Their exploits captured my imagination at an early age; even now at the threshold of war the desire to join their ranks proved irresistible. My goal was to be a fighter pilot. The fact that I had taken flying lessons in the summer of 1939, and had soloed; subsequently, graduating with a private pilot's license from the Civilian Pilot Training Program while in college strengthened my determination toward this goal.

Within days of the attack on Pearl Harbor I joined with a small group of teammates from the football team at Principia College in Elsah, Illinois, to travel to Ontario in order to join the Royal Canadian Air Force. This seemed the quickest way to become fighter pilots and a part of the forces rising to stem the Nazi juggernaut. We were welcomed by the RCAF recruiters, and assured that we would be kept intact as a group if we joined and were accepted. After being processed we were informed that we were all acceptable, but that there was a technical problem involved with one of the group whose father was a naturalized citizen of the United States. He would need a copy of his naturalization papers before he could be sworn in as a cadet of the RCAF. Since we had agreed that we would enlist enmasse or not at all we reluctantly returned to college to try to acquire the necessary document. Once back on campus, however, the disheartened group lost its impetus and disintegrated.

Although disappointed at the results of my first effort to enter service midst the company of friends, I began to look for other opportunities. I soon learned that the

Marine Corps was accepting and processing applicants for their Officer Corps at the Federal Building in St. Louis. Reasoning that once accepted I could transfer to their Air Arm after establishing my flying experience background, I reported the next day, and was run through the details of examination and processing. They told me that I had passed muster and was qualified for training at Quantico, Virginia, but that I would be required to return to college to await a formal letter of appointment to the Corps. Enthused I returned to college to spend the next week or two pestering the U. S. Post Office for delivery of the expected letter. Again I was destined for disappointment. Instead of the appointment, I received a letter informing me that "due to an overload of acceptable candidates" my turn for appointment could not possibly be processed and tendered before a year's lapse of time. Chastened but even more determined I called at the nearest Army recruiting office to try the same line of action I had planned with the Marines, but again I was told that all enlistments had been suspended for thirty days in order to handle the growing backlog of enlistments caused by the tragedy at Pearl Harbor.

By now discouragement was beginning to blunt my self-confidence and I began to worry about being drafted and perhaps never getting an opportunity to apply for air training. But as in so many times in life, opportunity knocked in the depths of my mental doldrums. A close friend, R. T. Bond, told me that in his home town, Little Rock, Arkansas, an Air Corps traveling board was processing applicants for cadets in the Army Air Corps, and he wanted me to go with him to try for it. In an instant all past disappointments were forgotten as I began preparations to leave with my friend for Arkansas. At Little Rock we handed over our required documents, met the board, took our physicals and completed the other processing details. At the end of the day we were called into a room with other applicants, and informed that we had been accepted as Aviation Cadets in the Army Air Corps Flying Training Program. After receiving congratulations from the board we were sworn into service, and instructed to return to our homes to put our affairs in order preparatory to receiving written orders from the Air Corps. By the end of December I had received orders directing me to report for duty at Williams Army Air Force Base, Chandler, Arizona.

My parting from my mother and sister Gayle was charged with poignant unspoken sadness as we each realized there was no way of knowing when we would be together again as a family, if ever. Later, in reflection, I often found added strength in the memory of the faith, confidence and courage displayed by my mother and sister as they watched the youngest member of the family leave for war. With the emotional wringout of departing over I left on a prearranged ride with a friend of many years standing, Jack Gordon, who was driving to California. I rode with him as far as Williams AAFB, my first duty station.

Arriving at the air base I found that I had become Aviation Cadet 17052391 assigned to G Company. The three or four weeks of basic training I was to spend here consisted mainly of orientation lectures, physicals and medical immunity shots, close order drill, lots of physical exercise, and the issue of a single pair of fatigue coveralls which turned out to be the standard uniform of the day, or night, at the Cadet Training Reception Center. About the time we began to wonder where they kept the airplanes we received orders to report to the Training Base at Santa Ana, California. With zooming spirits Bond and I cadged a ride with a colleague who owned a car, and departed eagerly for what we thought would be, "The Wild Blue Yonder." By ten o'clock the next evening we were approaching the outskirts of Santa Ana when we were exposed inadvertently to the other side of the coin of military flying. A highway patrolman loomed up before our headlights, flagging us to the side of the road where he told us to park with our lights out, and to sit tight. We jumped out of the car to find out what was up and instead we found out what was down. As an ear-splitting explosion reverberated out of the gathering darkness we all flopped instinctively to the ground. Later we found it was 90-mm antiaircraft firing in an air-raid scare. No harm was done, but as fledgling Aviation Cadets we began to realize that it was "not all beer and skittles" in the "wild blue yonder," and but for the grace of God that could be us up there under different circumstances, and probably would be sometime in the future in a different sky. In spite of it all, we survived our first brush with combat and proceeded to Santa Ana.

After the usual processing, which this time included issuance of uniforms, Santa Ana turned out to be a glorified repetition of Williams with a little more icing. We once again marched, studied, exercised, listened to lectures but still, once again, no airplanes! I was beginning to believe that the idea that we had any airplanes in our Army Air Corps was nothing but a vicious rumor perpetuated by the enemy. After we arrived a new policy was instituted requiring all cadets to take aptitude exams designed to determine their future flying training as toward pilot, navigator, or bombardier status. This gave us a few bad moments until we learned that we were exempt from this requirement since we had been accepted specifically for pilot training. Within a week or two orders were posted on the company bulletin board showing Flight School assignments of cadets in our company. With pleasure I found my name along with others posted to report to Cal-Aero Flying Academy, Ontario, California, for instruction in Primary Flight School. We eagerly turned in all non-essential equipment, cleared the base, and were bundled into buses for the trip to Cal-Aero.

Cal-Aero was a civilian-operated flying school contracted to provide flying programs to Aviation Cadets through Primary and Basic phases. All flight instructors and personnel were civilian except for the flight check pilots who were Army Air Corps Flying Officers. As new cadets we found ourselves assigned to the class of 42-I with the Stearman, PT-13, as our training aircraft. With my previous flying time I experienced little or no problems in the Primary course, and my instructor, a Mr. MacGregor, recognizing this, allowed me more freedom and time in learning aerobatic and formation flying than my flightmates. Primary flight training in general consisted of learning the coordinated movement required to control an aircraft under any and all conditions, and in developing judgment of depth perception and the relative speed difference between two or more flying objects. Anything beyond this in aerobatic or formation was like money in the bank to an aspiring fighter pilot. I took full advantage of the extra time allowed me by my flight instructor to upgrade my experience level in these bread and butter skills of the fighter pilots trade. After two or three months we were given Army flight checks, and those of us that passed were sent on to Basic Training in BT-15s, or the Vultee Vibrator as we called it. Now in a heavier aircraft we concentrated mainly on an intensive course in basic instrument and formation flying. It was the basic instrument phase that began to weed out the weak sisters from our ranks, and although I found it much less than easy I was able to progress sufficiently to satisfy my check pilots, and was elated to be graduated on to Advanced flying training.

After spending approximately four months at Cal-Aero I received orders directing me to report to Luke Army Air Force Base, Phoenix, Arizona, for Single Engine Advanced Flying Training. I felt very fortunate and happy to get these orders for many of my friends received orders to go to Twin Engine Flight Training. This would have been a definite handicap to a hopeful fighter pilot. Twin engine training was considered to be the start of the path to a bombardment aircraft assignment. So, with hope soaring I left California.

Arriving at Luke I discovered I had been enjoying a relatively idyllic life of freedom at the civilian Cal-Aero. Now I had to return to the reality of strict military discipline, Army style. In short order the class of 42-I was shaped up and busily integrated into the flying program. Advanced flying emerged as a truly enjoyable experience. We perfected and gained more experience in the flying skills we had learned in the earlier phases of our instruction. About the only really new training we were required to master was aerial and ground gunnery. Everyone welcomed this as it reminded us of the purpose of our training. The new heavier and more powerful aircraft, the AT-6, was beautiful to fly, and we were given ample opportunity and flight time to become well grounded in all phases of flying. The only big source of suspense and anxiety now in every cadet's mind was the assignment he would get upon graduation. By now every cadet had developed a preference of one kind or another, and my strong desire to be a fighter pilot had grown stronger than ever.

On September 29, 1942, we graduated and became rated pilots with the rank of second lieutenant per Special Order 254 and Personnel Order 233. Within twenty-four hours we each received further orders which revealed our first duty assignment, and our greatest hopes and fears centered on these orders, for the type of unit to which we were sent would determine the type of aircraft we would fly in the war. Eager to find out if I had gotten a fighter assignment I tore open my orders, and breathed a sigh of relief as I found I had been posted to the 55th Pursuit Squadron, 20th Pursuit Group, at Paine Field, Everett, Washington.

Three other friends in my cadet barracks, Frank H. Tribbett, James J. Toth, and Charles G. Tison were also assigned to the 20th Group, and we left together for our first duty assignment. Arriving at Paine Field we checked in at Base Headquarters, and signed the officer's register; after which we were sent to the 20th Group Headquarters. There we were assigned to the 55th Pursuit Squadron, and at the end of our first day as fighter pilots we found ourselves in a bachelor officers quarters paired up in comfortable rooms. We all had the good fortune to be posted to the same flight. We were allowed to relax for the first few days while we became acquainted in the squadron and studied the technical manual of the P-39D, the operational aircraft of the squadron.

Soon we were in the midst of tactical training in preparation for eventual overseas combat assignment. With the lapse of a little time we begin to find ourselves and our niche in the scheme of things. Our first taste of tragedy, one of the bitter facts of our new calling, came unexpectedly on Thanksgiving Day. Toth, Tribbett, Tison and I were planning on having a dinner together to celebrate our new-found careers as well as Thanksgiving. Since Charlie Tison had been scheduled for a formation flight at 9:00 A.M. we all dressed in class A's, and took him down to the flight line to wait for him to fly the training mission before we left for town. Our spirits were high as we watched Charlie's flight take off. The flight leader started a normal wide circling turn to the left while climbing out to allow the following planes a chance to form up. His wingman flew into position easily, but the element leader lost ground to the outside with his wingman, and tried to slide back to the inside under the leader's wingman to catch up. In doing so he misjudged the distance between himself and the leader's wingman, and his prop chewed into the wingman's tail structure. We watched in mounting horror as the stricken wingman's P-39 gyrated into a sickening spin which ended in an eruption of flame and smoke on the ground. In a few minutes our former horror turned into stabbing grief as we learned the poor wingman was our friend, Charlie Tison.

Soon after the tragedy we learned that half of the new pilots were to be sent on detached duty to March Field in Riverside, California, to fly simulated support missions for Army maneuvers in progress near there. There also were persistent rumors that the 20th Group was to be converted to P-38s. Inasmuch as I wished to stay with single-engined fighters, I volunteered for duty with the March Field detachment, which was to be reassigned to other Fighter Groups following the maneuvers. Nearly all my close associates had chosen to stay at Paine so I now found myself forming new personal friendships among the other young officers of the detachment. The nucleus of the new circle of friends was Frank Q. O'Connor, an irrepressible Californian; Robert E. Goodnight, a Nevadan, and George M. Lamb of Utah. Within a short time our little group became tight-knit, and was destined to remain intact until almost the end of World War II. Of all the fond memories and experiences I accumulated during the war, the fondest and most valued are those of this close group of friends whose loyalty, dependability, and support helped me realize some of my finest moments in the years to come. We flew simulated strafing and dive-bombing missions over the ground force maneuvers for the next few weeks at March. More often than not O'Connor, Goodnight, Lamb, and I flew our missions together, and by the time we left March Field the four of us had subconsciously acquired that rare ability vital to the professional fighter pilot, the knack of flying as a team and thinking as one, regardless of who led the flight. We were now ready for serious training in the tactical employment of fighters, and fortune smiled upon us. The four of us received identical orders to report to the bombing and gunnery range at Tonopah, Nevada, for assignment to the 354th Fighter Group being formed there.

We reported to Headquarters of the 354th Fighter Group on January 21, 1943, and were assigned to the 356th Fighter Squadron commanded by Captain Charles C. Johnson. Captain Johnson was the only pilot in the Group at that time who had combat experience gained in the Philippines at the outbreak of the war, and we felt especially fortunate serving under him. But two weeks later tragedy struck again when Captain Johnson was killed while test-hopping a newly delivered fighter. It was typical of this fine officer that he insisted on personally wringing out all new aircraft before any of his squadron pilots were asked to fly them. It was a chastened lot of pilots that continued training under the new Squadron Commander, Captain R. D. Neece. Every pilot redoubled his effort and concentration in an attempt to dull the keen loss we all felt at the loss of Captain Johnson.

The first week in March 1943 the Squadron was moved to its own base at Santa Rosa, California, and once again we had a change in command. Captain Neece was relieved by Captain James H. Howard, a former Navy pilot who had received his Army Air Corps Commission in China with General Claire Chennault's famed Flying Tigers. The assumption of command by Howard gave the squadron a tremendous boost. The enthusiasm and eagerness kindled under Johnson burned brightly again, for here was a commander whose skill was legendary, and whose superior leadership was soon amply demonstrated. Howard initiated a program of training in mutual support tactics as practiced and proven in combat by the Flying Tigers in China. His insistence upon perfection resulted in an aggressive, well-tempered fighting squadron finely tuned to the anticipated conditions of actual combat. We were encouraged to engage one another in simulated individual as well as flight combat, and Howard flew constantly on many training missions with the entire squadron demonstrating and executing tactical air commands which enabled us to achieve a flexibility and proficiency seldom attained by a squadron still in its training phase. The dramatic proof of Howard's combat wisdom and his uncanny ability to impart it to others was soon to be demonstrated in the future by the tempering of our squadron in the crucible of sixteen months of continuous combat during which it was to compile the enviable record of 298 aerial victories over the enemy with but twenty-two pilots lost from all causes, training as well as combat. Jim Howard's main concern was centered on the unit and those that were a part of it, and seldom if ever about his own record or himself. It was small wonder that with such an outstanding leader the squadron and the entire 354th Group was destined to become one of the sharpest thorns in the side of the Luftwaffe.

Howard had a decided distaste for the paper-shuffling chores of the commanding officer on the ground, preferring to concentrate on the constant improvement of the air work of his pilots. Consequently, he shifted most of the paper work and housekeeping duties to his staff, but not the responsibilities. His style of operating gave the squadron a body of well-trained ground officers accustomed to using their own initiative, and personal satisfaction was heightened all around. The ground pounders gained a feeling of being vital to the squadron's operation while the pilots developed a respect and loyalty reserved only for those commanders who demonstrate by action their ability and prerogative to command in the air as well as from behind a desk.

Under these favorable conditions the squadron moved to Salem, Oregon, during the first week of June 1943. We spent about four months at Salem honing our flying skills, and our anticipation was keyed to a high pitch for the combat we felt sure lay in the near future. Speculation ran high as to where we would be sent for combat duty, and as to what specific aircraft we would fly. We were convinced we would kiss the old P-39 goodbye since according to intelligence reports its operational performance configuration fell short of combat requirements in both the Far East and European Theaters. There was a prevalent rumor that a new fighter, called a P-51 or Mustang, had been developed from the A-36 ground support fighter at the request of the British but we naturally assumed a newly untried group such as ours would be far down the list to get assignment of such highly prized equipment. But our eagerness to get a piece of the action was such by now that we would be happy to take our old beat-up P-39s into the middle of hell.

CHAPTER 2

A rash of leaves were suddenly granted to all personnel in the latter part of September, and in our stampede to use them no one gave a second thought to the meaning of such generosity of Group Headquarters. I took off in my car with a carload of pilots who I dropped off along the way to St. Louis, where I planned to visit my family. I had put two and two together by the end of my leave and began to suspect that the Group had been alerted for overseas shipment. That would explain why Howard had hinted that it would perhaps be a good idea to leave my car at home after this leave. Without telling my family the real reason I made some excuse to leave the car behind, and caught a plane for Salem.

My addition had been right on the button, for when I arrived back on base I found the squadron busy turning in equipment and packing and crating all other gear for overseas shipment. Our immediate destination was to be Camp Kilmer, New Jersey, an East Coast embarkation point where we would be examined, inoculated, stenciled, and stamped for overseas shipment.

An Eastern embarkation point indicated to me two possibilities as to our ultimate destination, North Africa or the European Theater; and it was my private hope that it would be Europe, for there the main event would be fought.

We spent four cramped but boisterous days on a troop train en route, and were finally disgorged tired but eager at Camp Kilmer. By now scuttlebutt had it that we would sail for "Merry Old England."

For the next week our duties were merely to get into line for countless medical orderlies and doctors armed with enormous hypodermics. The tedium of the daily camp routine and the less-than-lustrous recreational facilities available around Kilmer gave me a great inspiration. I decided that my flight was in dire need of a different kind of a shot in the arm. Accordingly I engineered a delicate coup through Group Headquarters which called for Temporary Duty in New York—in the form of a twenty-four-hour pass. The entire flight would be attending a "public relations function." I neglected to reveal that the said function resulted from a private call to Billy Rose's Diamond Horseshoe reserving a ringside table for twenty-five people. The Diamond Horseshoe, a flamboyant nightclub of the era, patronized of course by the "public" was naturally, in our eyes, the prime spot for "public relations." The arrangements completed, we congregated at the Diamond Horseshoe, and proceeded to neutralize our medical shots with shots from a more familiar bottle. We had a hilariously successful evening, dining and dancing with the girls of the floorshow whom the management, contrary to usual policy, had graciously permitted to fraternize. In fact, the party was such a huge success that the thought began to nibble at my mind that we might not be able to pay the mounting tab.

However, our relationship with the public had been so good that when the time came to settle our tab I was politely informed that the management and some of the regular clientele had already signed for our bill in a gesture of patriotic fervor. We accepted the proffered gesture with good grace and alacrity, tipped our waiter, solemnly formed ranks, saluted the assembled guests, and slowly weaved in exaggerated dignity out to waiting taxis amid thunderous applause from the crowded bistro. "A" Flight thus emerged as battle-hardened veterans of the "Battle of New York."

Our Group was soon taken to a Brooklyn dock where we boarded HMS *Athlone Castle,* a British passenger vessel. The pilots were quartered four to a stateroom, and assigned to the main dining salon for mess. Next morning at sea I rushed eagerly down to breakfast sporting a hearty appetite. But my appetite evaporated after the first bite of the first course served by the English waiter. The first course was an innocent-looking plate of white fish, which revealed itself to be raw! *Raw!* I didn't pause to debate the issue, which was foreordained, but plunged headlong for the nearest ship's rail to return the doubtful delicacy to the sea via the most expedient method. Later I managed to convince the waiter that my taste ran to the more provincial, and managed to take most of my remaining meals and keep them.

The Group spent the next two weeks aboard ship in a state of uneasy calm pricked occasionally by an awakening awareness of the nearing reality of combat. When not performing abandon-ship drills we lounged for the most part around our cabins or on deck, weather permitting, playing poker. In this popular pastime Lieutenant

Jim Lane, an easygoing South Carolinian, was an expert, a postgraduate of former GI service. He usually cleaned the lot of us, but we stood in line begging for a chance to knock heads with him. Old Jim would probably have wound up a millionaire if the convoy had made a few hundred more zigzags on the way over.

One night about ten o'clock the "abandon-ship" alarm rang, and I ran breathlessly up to my lifeboat station, buckling the straps of my Mae West. I was shocked to a standstill by an eruption of flame which climbed a brilliant yellow ladder ending in a mushroom of dulling redness in the night off our port beam. We all huddled in fearful expectation for over an hour listening to shrill whistles and frantically blinking communication lights flickering intermittently around the horizon.

No one knew what had happened or what was going to happen, and we were too fearful of the probable answers to ask. Later the activity of the lights died away, leaving the enigmatic mantle of blackness to frustrate our questioning eyes. The power of the unknown to excite and stimulate the imagination is awesome. If my experience was typical there wasn't much sack time logged the rest of the night. Everyone was vastly relieved one morning a few days later to find the ship at anchor in the safe roadstead of Liverpool, England. The immediate relaxing of the atmosphere among the Fighter Group personnel could almost be physically felt. Voices became brighter, and horseplay long absent became routine again as the jaunty character of a Fighter Group began to reassert itself.

A final crisis developed before disembarkation when the ship's captain informed Colonel Kenneth R. Martin, the Group commander, that our Squadron mascot, a white bull terrier smuggled aboard, would have to be disposed of before we were allowed to enter England. He must have seen the dog being exercised by one of the men on the trip over. Now, naturally, no one could be found that knew anything about a dog, so a shakedown inspection was scheduled to find him. The ingenuity of our men was no less than that of any first-class outfit. The dog simply vanished into thin air, not to reappear again until we were inside England en route to base.

After the fruitless search and a little haggling among the Allied brass, the ship moved to dockside and we prepared to disembark. As we were filing down the gangplank I saw a cargo net full of footlockers being lowered over the side, and noticed with high glee that one of the footlockers had an awful lot of holes punched in it. I prayed that the winch operator wouldn't drop the load too hard and bruise the dog. . . . Another interesting cargo was being off-loaded from the ship's forward cranes, and as I reached the dock I realized that they were the fuselages of P-51 fighters. Within minutes I had it on authority of the latest rumor that indeed these aircraft were supposed to be assigned to us. Rumor or not, it served as an excellent omen on the arrival of our fighter group in the European Theater of Operations.

The Group pilots boarded a dockside train which pulled out of the area leaving the rest of the Group and equipment still on the dock. Later I learned that the ground echelons and equipment were sent straight on to Boxsted Airdrome, our assigned base, in order to set up house, and to accept delivery of our fighter aircraft which were to be delivered immediately from the Depot at Blackpool. Meanwhile, we pilots were sent to Greenham Commons Airdrome in Berkshire so that we could cut our teeth on the P-51As used there by the 10th Recon Group.

Within a week every pilot was checked out and we entrained again. We were taken to Colchester where we were loaded into trucks and transported to Boxsted where we found that the rest of the Group had been busy readying the station for our arrival.

Boxsted had two 6000-foot runways with connecting taxiways and hardstand dispersal areas for aircraft on which stood the answer to our dreams: brand new P-51Bs. Each Squadron had for its own use a large hangar, engineering and operations building, and separate living area in which were numerous Nissen huts for its men and officers. The base also boasted an Officers Mess Club and Enlisted Mens Mess Club along, with a Hospital and Group Headquarters complex. It was all very comfortable, convenient and even picturesque only as the English countryside can be.

Our Squadron's flight commanders, O'Connor, Goodnight, Lamb, and I all bunked in one hut with Jim Howard, the Squadron CO, and Bob Brooks, our Operations Officer, plus a few assorted new pilots. This arrangement proved to be an excellent one for coordination and control of the squadron, enabling us to exercise flexibility and to respond instantly to any order handed to the squadron from Group.

Our first month in the ETO was spent flying our new P-51s on training missions over England. We concentrated on Squadron and Group control missions while practicing mutual support tactics with the traditional combat units of an element of two fighters, a flight of four, a squadron of sixteen, and a Group of forty-eight fighters. At the same time we developed and practiced the technique and deployment tactics necessary to provide protective escort to bombers.

We had arrived in England assigned to the Ninth Air Force which was in the process of moving to the ETO from North Africa. But the Eighth Air Force under General Ira C. Eaker had requested that we be assigned to them for Operations duty since our P-51Bs were the first long-range fighters available, and they were in urgent need of support for their heavy bombers operating beyond Holland.

The Ninth Air Force was reluctant to lose control of the P-51s, so we ended up under administration control of the Ninth, and operational control of the Eighth. We found this set-up made us much like distant-cousins of both commands, but child of neither. It was this unique arrangement which allowed me to fly an eventual ninety-six combat missions, when the established policy was a maximum fifty missions per fighter pilot. By the time the Ninth Air Force had determined their combat tour policy, they discovered that I had already flown two tours.

The 1st of December, 1943, dawned brightly—a pleasant change since fog and overcast is the rule in England during the fall and winter months, and we had become accustomed to flying in marginal weather. The airspace over England was crowded and the danger of collision was great. The clear sky was a good omen, for today we were to go on our first combat mission, a fighter sweep over Saint-Omer, designed to introduce us to German flak and enemy territory.

For this initial mission Eighth Air Force had sent us Lieutenant Colonel Don Blakeslee from the veteran 4th Fighter Group which had evolved from the Eagle Squadron composed of Americans flying with the British before our entry into the war. Colonel Blakeslee was to brief and lead us on this crucial flight. We had an early morning training mission during which Blakeslee observed us, but only in the briefing before the combat mission in the afternoon did we get our first close glimpse of this legendary pilot. He was of medium height and build, with wavy brown hair, and pinned you with a penetrating gaze from steel gray eyes which, if not accompanied by a smile, made one decidedly uncomfortable. He was all business and the business was killing. In the briefing he let us know that he was a master of his craft, and that he would brook nothing less than perfection from those who flew with him. We had worked hard to achieve radio and air discipline in our training, and now we began to understand why. Blakeslee left us with the impression that it would be far better to *not* return from the mission than to be the unfortunate flier guilty of a breach in radio or air discipline. I've often wondered which scared us the most on that first mission, meeting the Germans or displeasing Colonel Blakeslee? After briefing was concluded Blakeslee discussed the standard tactics to be used in the event of engagement with enemy aircraft. After emphasizing the mutual support positions and breaking movements he stressed the inflexible policy of American pilots in the case of head-on attack between fighters. There were only three permissible alternatives:

(1) Shoot down the enemy fighter or be shot down, (2) Make the enemy fighter break off attack first voluntarily, (3) Failing all else, fly through on collision course.

He stated in no uncertain terms that we *never*, repeat *NEVER*, turn away from head-on attack before the enemy! A period of pregnant silence followed his last sentence. Finally a young pilot in the front row hesitantly asked what would happen if the German pilot turned out to be as bullheaded as we were? A flicker of a smile creased Blakeslee's face as he replied, fixing his gray eyes on the uncomfortable young man, "In that case, son, you'll have earned your extra flight pay the hard way!" This broke up the briefing in more ways than one, and after being dismissed we all headed for our fighters to prepare for take-off, laughing in spite of our anxiety.

We taxied out to the assembly area at the end of the runway. I was leading my flight of four Mustangs, with Lieutenant Bob Klopotek on my wing. The bright sky of the morning had given way to frontal weather by noon, and now as I looked down the runway I couldn't see the end of it through the fog.

Blakeslee had said in briefing if the weather socked in we would take off in pairs, fly through the soup in a climbing turn to the left, and form up the group after topping the overcast. The plan was simple, but considering our inexperience it could become hazardous and complicated if we lacked the ability to fly sustained instruments long enough to penetrate the thick overcast. We ordinarily form up below the clouds, and set course to penetrate the overcast in tight formation on a strict heading without turns. But today the overcast was right down to the deck. We would be on instruments as soon as we became airborne. Every pilot who took off today would feel the cold play of fear, for no one took off blind in a fighter without fear unless he was too stupid and unimaginative to recognize the possible dangers involved. I took off when my turn came to go, with Bob Klopotek hugging my right wing. As I broke ground a thousand feet down the runway I did a little hugging myself as I held the Mustang down close to the runway to keep flying reference while pulling up the gear and flaps. After trimming up, I raised the nose, firmly established on instruments. I started a shallow turn to the left praying no one else would be in the airspace we'd be using. With my eyes glued to the needle, ball, and airspeed indicator we flew on and on for what seemed hours. My mental tension was mounting, and I was becoming pretty nervous wondering where in the hell the top was. I wanted to steal a peek to see if Klopotek was still with me, but I didn't dare take my eyes from the instruments lest I lose concentration and cause us both to spin out.

Just about the time I felt that I couldn't stand the suspense any longer we broke into clear visibility at 12,000 feet, and found those ahead of us circling in formation above the cloud deck. With infinite relief Klopotek and I joined them to wait for the rest of the Group as it emerged in pairs from the clouds below. Miraculously everyone made it up through the soup without untoward incident, and soon the entire Group was formed in orbit above the weather.

Blakeslee set course in the Lead Squadron for Holland across the Channel, and the other two squadrons flew into position on him. The high squadron took up station 500 feet higher abreast *down sun,* away from the sun's position, and the low squadron 500 feet lower abreast *up sun* or toward the sun's position which gave each better sight coverage of the other's sun blind side and rear. This enabled the entire Group to enjoy potential warning of attack from any quarter, and allowed the group leader to direct piecemeal interception so as to preserve his main force intact en route to the mission target where the bulk of his power was needed.

Each squadron was composed of four flights Red, White, Blue, and Green with four fighters in each flight; Red flight was usually led by the squadron commander. It was Green flight which was ordinarily considered the flexible one to be used in warding off any pre-target rendezvous attack by the enemy. Color designation of flights on a mission normally rotated among the permanent flight designations of A, B, C, and D in each squadron. The Green flight assignment on a mission was eagerly sought after by each flight commander since it was the most likely to get a crack at the enemy if they were contacted. The flight positions flown in squadron formation were essentially the same relative positions of those of the squadrons to each other in the group formation, nearly line abreast staggered up and away from the sun's position.

After crossing the Channel the group crossed into the coastline of Holland, flew inland about ten miles, then turned southwest, flying just inside the coastline over Flanders into France. Everyone in the group had his head swiveling like a searchlight looking for "bogies" (unidentified aircraft). No evidence of the enemy materialized, and the mission began to assume the familiar aspects of a routine training mission. We began to relax from the accumulated tensions of our first combat mission—but not for long. Suddenly ugly sporadic flak bursts appeared menacingly to the east of the formation. An apt reminder that the enemy knew we were over their territory.

As we approached the enemy coast a constant undulating whine developed in the radio earphones which continued throughout the flight over the Continent. Later we discovered that this was the effect of German radar on our radios as it scanned us to keep tabs on our location. It didn't interfere with our interplane transmissions, but it was eerie to be constantly reminded that the enemy below was following your every move. (A month or so later our receivers were modified eliminating this interference which did a lot for our nerves.)

An hour and a half after take-off we arrived back at base without casualty except for a flak hole Jim Lane collected from one of the bursts we had seen. The only real excitement on the mission came at landing when one of the group cut Colonel Blakeslee out of the traffic pattern, and the colonel informed one and all that "the next SOB that cut in front of him while landing was going to get an ass full of lead." Following this terse little announcement there wasn't a P-51 to be found in the pattern until Blakeslee had landed and taxied into his hardstand. In debriefing Colonel Blakeslee observed that considering all aspects of our first mission we might survive the war, providing we learned to land after missions in an orderly manner rather than the method of "God save the hindmost." For three days after our first mission on December 1 we flew further training missions over England practicing our air work, formation instruments, and needless to say working extra hard on landing pattern traffic control.

CHAPTER 3

On December 5 the Group was briefed and took off on a heavy bomber escort mission over Amiens, France. No enemy opposition other than intermittent light flak was evident. Our chief prey—German fighters—didn't materialize. We spent the day perfecting our screening tactics for protecting the bomber stream. I gained a new and deep respect for the bomber crews as I watched them plow doggedly through flak concentrations without wavering. As I watched this same display of perseverance almost daily in the months to come it became my firm conviction that bomber crews as a breed must be unrivaled for sheer guts and determination. Flak was the one danger we couldn't help them with, and from what I saw they simply ignored it, if that was possible. Due to their massiveness bombers couldn't make quick and erratic maneuvers so they took a calculated risk and flew straight on course through the black hell. The action was inspiring and impressive to an escorting fighter, and I have entertained nothing but genuine admiration for bomber crews since. Our second mission ended as another milkrun—a term we came to use describing missions with no claims, no losses, and no enemy action. I began to wonder where the enemy fighters were hiding.

The next combat mission was escort duty again for heavy bombers over Emden, Germany. To keep our experience on a par, the flight lead was rotated among Goodnight, O'Connor, Lamb, myself, and other pilots in the flight, and I did not participate in this mission. This time, naturally, the Group sighted the first German opposition, which however was driven off with only threatening action. The Group returned intact except for one plane of the 353rd which had run into either flak or engine trouble, and was reported missing in action. This was our first casualty, and it had a sobering effect on every member of the Group re-emphasizing the deadly seriousness of our job. Even more pronounced was the grim determination of each pilot to carve a piece of revenge from the first German fighter available.

Generally a fighter group consists of three fighter squadrons with each assigned twenty-five to thirty operational aircraft. A squadron has seventy-five to eighty fighter pilots along with the necessary ground crew, administrative, and service personnel to operate autonomously if need be, but usually they operate in concert under control and command of a group headquarters organization. For the average combat mission each squadron is required to provide four flights of four manned aircraft for the group effort with an extra flight of four aircraft and pilots on stand by status ready to fill any operational gaps created before take-off by chance aborts among the assigned mission aircraft or pilots. This standard operating procedure effectively molds a combat group mission striking force of forty-eight coordinated fighters to carry out its assigned task.

Now I began to discover some of the less enjoyable duties of a flight commander when on the ground. It was my responsibility to provide the squadron commander and operations officer with one stand by and four pilots to man fighters for every combat mission. By now my pilots were all clamoring to fly every mission, and I could easily have used all sixteen planes flown by the squadron. The other three flights were as eager as my own; so each commander was forced to set up a strictly impartial system of rotation in the interest of fair play—and self preservation. . . .

The flight commander was expected to lead his flight every two out of three missions, reserving one mission to provide lead experience for his element leaders so they would be qualified to assume command of the flight if necessary. Thus I enjoyed the privilege of flying more combat than the average pilot. Occasionally the squadron commander rotated the squadron lead with his flight commanders, and the group commander rotated the group lead with his squadron commanders for the same purpose. In effect all pilots were being continually offered experience one step above their basic duty. This system proved itself to be excellent in practice as well as theory, for never during the war did the group or its squadrons become less effective as a fighting force due to the loss of key personnel.

December 13 dawned overcast, but we were informed the weather was clearing toward Kiel, where we were to provide support and cover for heavy bombers. The clearing weather over target was welcome news, but the take-off on instruments and group penetration meant a tense forty minutes for everyone. Only the group leader and squadron commanders were actually on full instruments; everyone else was flying formation on them; but every pilot had to be ready to go on instruments himself in case worsening visibility broke up the formation contact. Rapid transition from formation to the gauges was difficult procedure at best. No matter how much experience you accumulated on instruments the fear of the unknown factor which could cause a group melee always rode with you during these mass weather penetrations.

We emerged from the overcast on course, and proceeded to Kiel where the group deployed for bomber stream coverage. There were around five hundred bombers in the stream, and we with forty-eight Mustangs, as the only escort over target were spread pretty thin to cover them all. We split up the flights into basic elements of two aircraft to gain more coverage, and I began to hear bogie reports over Radio-Transmissions. The bogies were identified as ME-110s, and I could tell by the RT that they were being engaged by some one of our fighters who in their excitement failed to locate the attack in relation to the bombers for the rest of us. Consequently most of the group darted around fruitlessly in their own patrol areas searching for the enemy. As it turned out the Germans had made a half-hearted attempt to reach the bombers, but had fled at the attack of the first two Mustangs which charged them. A few strikes of armor piercing incendiaries were observed on one Messerschmitt, but no damage was noted other than heavy trailing smoke. This was counted later as the group's first combat contact—a "possible" rather than a "destroyed."

Everyone accompanied the bombers longer than scheduled hoping that the Germans would show up again. But thirty minutes after the P-47s arrived for withdrawal support we finally gave up hope. The P-47s kept mistaking us for ME-109s, so we were ordered by the group commander to return to base before we were forced to fire in self-defense. I knew that the Group would be returning to England like a swarm of bees. Having no desire to let down in the soup over England with so much company I dived to the deck with my wingman on the way back planning to strafe airfields and rail traffic before we reached the Channel. We found slim pickings on the way out except for one freight engine which we left spurting steam two hundred feet into the sky. Coming to the Channel I found the overcast had lowered visibility to the point where I had to fly partially by instruments and partially by surface glare from the sea. I was greatly relieved when I saw the English coast slide into view faintly etched below in the haze. I reduced altitude to within fifty feet of the ground, where I found the visibility slightly improved, and after flying a square search pattern for a few minutes we stumbled onto our base. The mission had taken four hours, and we were really pooped when we reported for debriefing, and gladly took the relaxing ounce of "mission whiskey" offered by the flight surgeon.

I was very disappointed at not being able to get into the action with the ME-110s, but it was good to know the enemy had at last been contacted. However, the bad weather that I had encountered while returning evidently had claimed a victim, for one of the Group's fighters was reported missing in action. The Officers' Club was subdued that night, for so far the boxscore was against us, two lost against one "possible destroyed."

Three days later we were up early, and were briefed for a penetration support of heavy bombers over Bremen. It was hazy over England but with no actual overcast, and the forecast was clear over the Continent; we took off and set course in good spirits, hoping to catch the Luftwaffe this time. We rendezvoused with the bomber stream over Holland, and deployed as cover escort. Bogies were reported fifteen minutes later.

Everyone switched on gunsights, and raised their power settings for combat, and started searching expectantly for German fighters. Sounds of battle engagement broke over the RT again as ME-109s and JU-88s were identified by flights of the 355th Squadron on the other side of the bomber stream. Of all the lousy luck! We were on the wrong side of the bombers again, and although we watched sharply for a wandering German, none appeared in our sector, and we remained spectators with nothing to shoot at. The only excitement in our tedious patrol occurred when occasionally a nervous bomber gunner lobbed 50-caliber tracers at us, mistaking us for 109s. We were used to this since we realized our silhouette resembled that of the German 109. Cheering news crackled over the RT, however, announcing that Lieutenant Charles F. Gumm of the 355th had shot down an ME-109, and that someone had damaged a JU-88.

We were elated at the first definite kill of the Group, but were chagrined at being unable to participate ourselves. When the withdrawal-support fighters showed up, we charged furiously for the deck intent on clobbering anything that moved between us and the Channel. It was a peculiar assortment of strafing targets reported later at debriefing.

During the balance of December the 354th Fighter Group flew five more bomber-escort missions of which I flew three. My bad luck held, and I missed the best fight five days before Christmas where the Group destroyed four ME-110s and got two probables, and damaged four more—but at a loss of three pilots and planes. Our first month of combat ended with a score of eight kills versus seven losses. The balance wasn't spectacular, but at least it was slightly in our favor now. We were beginning to come to grips with the enemy, and we knew that we could more than hold our own, given the opportunity. Furthermore we received reports from Bomber Command that the introduction of the Mustang as a target-support aircraft had lifted bomber crew morale to a new high and they definitely felt that enemy fighters were less of a menace than before. All in all, this was a very gratifying response to our efforts.

The group had no combat missions from January 1 through January 3, and I had my crew chief, Staff Sergeant Clint Thompson, set my fighter, AJ-T, up in the gunnery abutment so my armorer, Sergeant Tracy, and I could boresight my 50-caliber machine guns in at 100 yards instead of the usual 1500 feet. I had heard Colonel Blakeslee say once that to get a sure kill you had to fly right up their butt, and chew it off at close range. I knew if anyone had the answers he did, and I intended to follow his advice.

On January 4 we flew a target-support and withdrawal for the heavies again, and it was the same old story. A small fight developed someplace away from my patrol sector in which a German was knocked down, and we lost a Mustang, but by the time I got there it was all over and the Germans had gone. I couldn't seem to get near a German fighter.

The next day was another typical winter day over England—thick haze under a high overcast. However, at briefing the weather officer reported clear forecast over the target, Kiel. Intelligence reported that there were indications that the Germans had moved large forces of rocket carrying ME-110s into the airfield complex of northern Germany. It was assumed that this movement was a reaction to the intensive bombing we had given the area during the past month. We expected stiff opposition from these night fighters. We manned our planes in eager anticipation, with the knowledge that there was a high probability of heavy enemy engagement on the mission. Our squadron commander, Major Jim Howard, had been designated Group leader for the mission, and I was leading Green flight of the lead squadron—an excellent opportunity to meet the enemy in combat.

Howard led the Group unerringly to rendezvous twenty miles west of Kiel. He deployed the 355th and 353rd Squadrons to the rear and the sides of the bomber stream and led our squadron forward past the lead bomber division for deployment screening of the bombers spearhead. I'm sure Howard expected, as I did, that the main enemy attack would develop at this point, for the bomber firepower was the weakest and most vulnerable from this quarter of attack. We proved correct in this assumption. As we pulled a mile or two in front, we could see a string of twin-engined formations about five miles out coming at the bombers in a head-on attack. We were slightly higher and to the left of the oncoming Messerschmitts, in perfect position to hit them in a quartering attack from the front, but Howard had a different idea. He knew the least dangerous attack would be the obvious one, but he reasoned that a frontal attack would enable some of the enemy planes to slip through to the bombers with their rockets. So he held the squadron on course parallel with the approaching ME-110s, in echelon formation to the right, instructing each flight commander to peel off to the right as he passed an enemy formation in a driving attack up the rear of their formation, thus scattering each enemy formation and breaking up their concentrated line of attack. We had learned that when German forces were broken up like this, the ranging Mustang elements around the bomber stream had little trouble in picking them up before they could get to the bombers.

Howard's tactical plan worked to perfection. As the flight nearest to the passing enemy I peeled off for the first attack. Leaning into a diving right turn, I radioed my wingman, the element leader and his wingman to pick separate enemy elements, and to attack line abreast individually in order to give everyone a chance for a kill, and to break up the enemy flight completely. Now I concentrated on the rearmost plane of an enemy flight ahead. I could see the muzzle flash blinking at me as the rear gunner wrestled to keep his 7-mm machine gun on me, but ducking my Mustang below his ship, I used his tail empennage as a shield and blind spot of approach to get to point blank range. I retarded my throttle to avoid overrunning the slower ME-110 and coordinated the controls until I had my sights fixed in a slightly quartering attack on the fuselage just above his wing root. I squeezed off a short burst, and was amazed to see strikes bursting and lighting up the enemy craft from its wingtip to its tail. The Messerschmitt exploded into a flaming torch spewing thick masses of oily black smoke which engulfed my plane completely. As I pulled up out of the smoke, I found myself under the leading ME-110 which was breaking away to the left in an effort to escape our attack. Throwing a quick glance around the sky, I pursued the lead plane. In that glance I saw the German flights exploding in every direction, my Mustangs hard on the tails of those surviving the first attack. Those already hit were marked by lengthening splashes of fire and smoke which trailed like four or five limp fingers etched in sharp relief against the clear blue sky. I clamped on to the tail of the ME-110 ahead of me, and tripped the trigger of my 50-calibers again as the pip settled on the canopy. Again the brilliant display of API (armor piercing incendiary) strikes began to play brightly around the fuselage and up and down the wings of the hapless twin-engined fighter, and soon I was choking on black acrid smoke from the booming fire which erupted from his fuel tanks. As the Messerschmitt fell off in an arching ball of flame, I pulled up and around adjusting my throttle and prop settings for a climb. I was surprised to find the sky practically empty, where before there had been hundreds of aircraft. It was a lonely and exposed feeling, and I searched for a friendly single-engined fighter with which to join forces. Finally I saw one high overhead flying in the direction of the bomber stream that could just barely be seen far to the north. Assuming the fighter to be a combat-dispersed Mustang like myself I commenced a maximum climb to join him before arriving back at the bomber stream. Relieved to find company so easily, I kept sweeping the area around us for enemy aircraft, not paying much attention to the fighter above. Fortunately for me I was climbing in an area which was blind to his line of sight. As I came up almost level and a little to his rear about a thousand feet away I realized with a shock that it was a German plane—an ME-109. Evidently the 109 pilot got his first sight of me at the same instant, for he whipped the 109 into a violent wingover to the left and splitessed for the deck. I rolled over and followed, determined to get revenge for my own stupidity. Halfway down I overtook him, but the excessive speed we were building made it difficult to control the ship for sighting. I kept squeezing off short bursts at every opportunity, but was only able to observe a few random strikes and no visible damage. Soon my plane began to vibrate and buck, demanding all of my attention to attempt recovery, as the ground was coming alarmingly near for a vertical dive position. I remember the shock of seeing the ME-109 shed its wings below me as I struggled to move the stick from the neutral position. Reaching for the elevator tab control wheel on the left of the cockpit seat, I eased it backward, and the plane responded, easing out of the headlong dive. The near terminal velocity and the added "g" forces caused the plane to buck even harder. I looked out at the wings hoping they would hold, and saw what appeared to be 3 or 4 inch waves in the metal skin, undulating from the wing root outward to the tip. I could hardly believe my eyes, and quickly looked away. The struggling Mustang bottomed out in its dive with only a few short feet remaining between us and the ground. We were traveling so fast that my eyes only recorded an impression of flashing treetops as I whipped into a screaming climb for altitude and safety. Regaining control of the plane and my courage I set climb for the bomber stream once again looking for companionship. Eventually I found Jim Howard in his Mustang *Ding Hao* headed for home with a wingman. I joined up, content to let Jim do all the work en route through haze and soupy weather.

But my troubles were not yet over. As we crossed over the Frisian Islands in the North Sea we could see a tremendous weather build up to the west over England. Like most fighter pilots Jim preferred to fly under weather instead of over it whenever possible, and when he rocked his wings I knew we were going to duck beneath the weather to avoid the congestion of returning bombers and fighters which would be competing for let down space through the cloud layers over England. Jim's wingman and I tucked into close formation with him, and we started our let down out over the North Sea where we had some elbow room.

After forty or fifty minutes of flying we discovered the haze extended right down to the deck, and Jim gingerly felt for the surface, reducing his rate of descent. I was flying within three feet of Howard's wing, with my eyes glued to his wingtip. We were in a thick milky haze with practically no forward visibility. Suddenly without warning Jim's Mustang pulled upward and disappeared. Looking forward I saw the glare of water which because of my angle of flight appeared to be above me. My instinct had caused me to automatically pull back on the stick when Jim pulled up, and this had saved me from flying straight into the surface of the sea. Within seconds I broke through a cloud layer into a band of clear horizontal visibility where I found Jim and his wingman. We rejoined formation, and headed southwest between the cloud layers hoping to find a break over England.

According to our elapsed flying time we knew we must be quite close to land. Soon we received a strong voice signal which gave us a steer to base, and knew we were almost home. Finding no holes, we again set up for a slow groping let down. This time we were lucky for the visibility was great enough to navigate at five hundred feet, and Jim quickly found Boxsted. Howard dipped his wing for us to form echelon right, and we peeled off for landing.

At debriefing we found the group had enjoyed its biggest day. We had destroyed eighteen German aircraft, and damaged five without loss to ourselves. Since I had no film of the ME-109 incident, I claimed only the two ME-110s; so our actual score should have been nineteen destroyed. We were told that the bombers sustained no losses due to enemy fighter action on this mission which doubled our jubilation. The whole mission is a demonstration of Jim Howard's amazing abilities. He was able to size up the situation, decide instantly on the best tactics, and exercise control of his forces in order to execute the tactics desired. He is in my mind the finest air commander ever to fly in combat. The group like well-trained hunting hounds had now been blooded and victorious, and had a firm confidence in its own capabilities, operating from now on with professional dependability.

On December 7 we flew another escort mission to Ludwigshafen in southern Germany—a milkrun. We encoun-

1. My portrait in uniform, September 1942.

2. The invasion of Billy Rose's Diamond Horseshoe in New York, November 1943, just before leaving Camp Kilmer, New Jersey, for England. Left to right: George Barris, Mack O. Tyner, Richard Payne, Harry Fisk, myself, Frank Q. O'Connor, Bob Goodnight, George "Stud" Hall, Earl Depner. Bob Welden, George Lamb and Bob Shoup. These 12 pilots shot down a total of 64 German aircraft, as eight of them became aces. Five were killed and one taken prisoner.

3. We expected less, but the 354th Fighter Group was given brand-new North American P-51B Mustangs, originally designed for the RAF.

4. Max Lamb, 7½ victories.

5. Bob Goodnight, 7¼ victories.

6. Myself.

7. Frank O'Connor, 10½ victories.

8. Jim Howard, 6 victories, 356th F.S. and Group Commander.

10. Colonel Kenneth R. Martin, our first Group Commander, 5 victories. He parachuted into German captivity after a head-on collision with an Me-109 on February 11, 1944.

9. Colonel George Bickel

tered nothing but flak, and we returned with no kills, no losses.

January 11 brought typically overcast weather. At briefing we found the day's target to be bomber escort over Halberstadt about fifty miles southwest of Berlin, and the consensus was that we should flush some enemy fighters on this one since it was right in the middle of their playground. Everyone was keyed up as they manned their planes for take-off. We set course and flew without incident to rendezvous under the overcast at 25,000 feet. This mission the bombers were at 17,000 feet instead of their usual altitude of 25,000 feet. We were in the process of deploying the squadrons about the area when someone exclaimed over the RT, "My God! There are Germans coming up in droves beneath the bombers!" Looking down we could see ME-110s and ME-109s climbing like a swarm of bees from the deck. They seemed to come from all directions about 10,000 feet below the bomber stream. The voice on the RT cried, "Go down and get the bastards!" I wasn't sure but the voice sounded enough like Major Howard's to satisfy us, and instantly Mustangs were raining upon the climbing Messerschmitts. The squadron dived so quickly, spreading out and picking individual prey, that we unintentionally blocked Howard's diving path making him pull up in order to keep from chewing our tails off. The whole group had dived to the attack, and Howard knew someone ought to stay with the bombers even if it had to be him alone, so he climbed back up to ride herd on the bombers, more than a little annoyed at our helter-skelter attack.

When I heard the command to go get them, I, like everyone else, wheeled over in a dive for the nearest

ME-110 flight I could see, without giving a second thought. On the way down Frank O'Connor was right with me, so we spread out a little, each taking half of the flight. The enemy saw us coming and turned away splitting their flight in two, one element fleeing to the northeast and the other to the northwest. I lined out for those going northeast, and Frank took off after the others. In a couple of seconds I pulled up under my prey, retarded my throttle a bit, and coasted up in a climbing attack from eight o'clock on the nearest Messerschmitt. There was again the immediate flare of multiple API strikes all over the craft as I fired, and fire engulfed the fighter instantly. Pulling in line with the second 110 I opened fire again observing miniature strike bursts run quickly from the wingtip toward the fuselage, but at this instant I became aware of an object coming in at me from two o'clock high. It was a single ME-109 boring in at me with guns blinking. I turned my P-51 away from my target to meet the 109 in a head-on firing pass, and as my tracers arched toward him the 109 turned away and rolled over for the deck, and as he pulled through for his dive I scored a few strikes in his empennage. I had turned back to finish off the 110, when I heard Frank O'Connor calling me over the RT. It seemed he had encountered a similar experience. His 109, however, had two friends along, and the three of them ended up chasing Frank around in a "Lufbery Circle" trying to "shoot his ass off" as Frank put it. I asked his location, but Frank had no idea how to tell me. All he could say was that he was going around and around in tighter circles with three ME-109s. I careened around for four or five minutes at full bore in a frantic effort to find O'Connor. It was one of the most agonizing few minutes I have ever spent in the air, and the most frustrating. Finally I heard Frank's voice over the RT saying, "Never mind, Dick, I finally caught the SOB's and shot one of them down. The other two cowardly bastards ran away." What a nut! Here I was practically blowing up my engine over Germany hunting for him, and it turns out he's casually having a turkey shoot. Grinning and concealing my former enormous concern from the crazy Irishman I told him it was time to start home, as the bomber stream had long since returned.

I cast around for a few minutes until I picked up a Mustang for company, and then set course for home. On the way home a single ME-410 appeared suddenly 20 feet above us running for home in the opposite direction. The German was as surprised as we were, and bent his throttle forward pouring a great volume of black exhaust from his engine stacks. I started instinctively to turn for attack, but not knowing the state of fuel aboard the accompanying Mustang which was from another squadron, I thought better of it and reset our course for home.

Heading toward England I began to think about all the Jerry targets I had passed up trying to find Frank, and decided to claim a drink per target from him at the club that night. I could almost hear his outraged cry, "What d'ya mean I owe you five drinks!" I chuckled all the way back to England thinking about how O'Connor would holler about the drinks.

After landing at debriefing we discovered the group had racked up another big day. The group as a whole had destroyed fifteen enemy planes and damaged sixteen. A good day's work, with no losses. Jim Howard came in with three destroyed claims and three damaged, which was quite a feat. Within twenty-four hours a big stir was caused when Eighth Air Force Headquarters requested that we re-examine our claims to find the name of the pilot who had attacked thirty German planes alone, driving them all off, and destroying six, by confirmation of the incredulous bomber crews who had witnessed the feat. They said that the Bomber Command was determined to find out who this pilot was. It didn't take long to find out that our shrinking violet was none other than Major Jim Howard who had been so unceremoniously cut out of the pattern on the way down to the attack on the climbing German thrust from below. Jim had returned to the bombers just as they came under attack by thirty ME-109s, and in an unequaled display of tactical aggressiveness proceeded to run off every German in the sky shooting down six of the thirty. According to the bombers, not one of the Germans was able to attack before they were chased from the area by the wildman in a Mustang marked AJ-A. This incident drew wide acclaim from the Army Air Force, and to me it was visible proof of the conviction I had long held that Howard was an airman of superior abilities. I was overjoyed to see Jim get the recognition he had long deserved, for he was a quiet man who normally shied from personal publicity. Our "one man Air Force" deservedly was recommended for and received the Congressional Medal of Honor.

A few days later, on the 15th of January, Howard was promoted to lieutenant colonel as squadron commander, and I along with the other flight commanders in the squadron, was promoted to captain.

On January 29 we escorted heavy bombers over Frankfurt where the 355th found and latched onto the only

Jerries in sight knocking down five of them with one "probable" and four "damaged." The rest of us scurried around and found nothing to shoot at. We returned home with no losses. Competition for victories between squadrons began to grow.

The group took off on January 30 on an escort mission for Brunswick, a good hot area for German fighters. After deployment I was leading my flight on a sweep of the sector when I saw an ME-109 three or four miles north of the bomber stream 5000 feet below us attacking a straggling B-17 which somehow had strayed from the others. I whipped into a dive, trying to reach the B-17 before he was shot down. Lieutenant Mack Tyner was my wingman, and Captains Bob Goodnight and Max Lamb were my element. Like old pros they stayed with me in perfect tactical formation as we dove for the two planes. Halfway down the B-17 burst into flame, and fell to earth—spilling chutes. As the pilot of the ME-109 paused to watch the falling B-17 I had enough time to reach him, pull out of my dive, and line up my sight pip. I waited a second until his wingspan filled my gunsight so as to have a sure hit. I held the trigger down for a long hard burst which sent 75 to 100 API's tearing into the 109. My range must have been near perfect, for the craft literally blew up in my face. Usually when I shot down a plane, I secretly hoped the pilot would be able to bail out, but for the first time I had a real desire to kill an enemy pilot.

As we turned to climb back to the bombers I discovered a JU-88 tooling along about 1000 feet below us heading west toward the Channel, oblivious evidently to all the world just as if he were on a Sunday crosscountry jaunt.

Mack Tyner had been bemoaning the fact that he never got a chance to get a victory as a wingman, so I decided that this was a good safe chance for him to get one. I called the flight over the RT, and pointed the JU-88 out at two o'clock low. I told Mack it was all his, and that Goodnight, Lamb, and I would fly cover for him while he picked it off. Tyner rolled over, and dived behind the JU-88 ending up too far behind and out of range. I called to him to hurry up and close in so the rear gunner wouldn't have so much time to aim. Tyner was taking so much time that I began to worry. I told him to dive under the Jerry and make a climbing attack from beneath —a safer approach. Then I heard Bob Goodnight say, "Who the hell is that 88 shooting at?" Looking up, I saw to my horror that 20-mm shells from the Jerry's forward cannon pod were bursting all around a P-51 that was cruising along in front of it. Forgetting Tyner, Goodnight and I dove on the 88. I got there first and tripped my 50s, but only one gun fired, making it difficult to aim them properly. Finally, by riding the rudder, I scored some strikes along the tail and fuselage which drew the pilot's attention away from the P-51. The 88 made a diving turn for a low cloud bank when he saw me and Goodnight riding his tail. We let him go to find out who the pilot was in the P-51. He turned out to be our old buddy Lamb who hadn't even known he was being shot at. To this day I don't understand how "Lambie-pie" got out in front of that JU-88.

When we arrived back at base we were all so glad that Lamb was safe that we couldn't chew him out for giving us a scare. Besides, he was as good a pilot as any of us, so there was nothing to say. Poor old Mack Tyner didn't get his Jerry, and I told him later if he wasted that much time setting up a kill he'd be fifty years old before he became an ace. At debriefing we found that the Group had had only a respectable day, not a good one. Howard had gotten a kill which, with mine, accounted for two. Bradley, Eagleston, and Dalglish of the 353rd had gotten one apiece bringing the group score for the day to five kills. There were two probables and ten damaged, including our JU-88. The best news of the day was that we again had no losses.

This mission ended our second month of combat during which the group had completed eighteen missions of which I had flown eleven, and I had contributed four of the total fifty-three kills. Group losses were eleven planes and pilots, none of which fortunately had been from our squadron—the statistic I was most proud of.

On February 1, Frank O'Connor and I got a three day pass to explore London. We dressed in our most presentable Class A uniforms, wheedled a few loans from among our less fortunate comrades, arranged transportation into Colchester from the squadron transportation officer, and caught the train for London.

Arriving in Victoria Station we hailed a cab, and proceeded to what one of our friends had called a private hotel, recommending it highly. Upon registering we were politely informed that for £5 apiece we would have the second floor suite with breakfast for ourselves and guests. Up in the suite Frank wondered what they had meant by guests? I told him that the word meant the same thing here as it did in the U.S., and Frank pointed out the fact that we didn't know anyone in London to invite as guests for breakfast. I ventured that the English evidently had ample confidence in the gregarious nature of American pilots since there had evidently been a few here before us. At any rate, freshly scrubbed and armed with hope, Frank and I set out for the pubs. We investigated every female available in every spot we hit, with a date for the evening's festivities in mind, but our every tactic was expertly countered.

We ended up the evening congregating with other luckless pilots, trying hard to drink the pubs dry, and telling one another how our unit was ridding the skies of the Luftwaffe. The stories were usually interrupted at least once a night while we dove under the nearest table to wait out an air raid—a peculiarly frequent performance for a Luftwaffe that had been chased from the skies so often. Little inconsistencies like this didn't bother us a bit, and the stories became more exaggerated as the night went on. As a rule we ended up in our suite like the good boys our mothers firmly believed us to be, sleeping through those wonderful breakfasts that had been so generously offered with our lodgings. In fact, on the train back to base Frank made the astute observation that, "If this war lasts long enough those people are going to become millionaires on unserved breakfasts!"

While Frank and I were on leave the group and squadron had flown three missions collecting another kill, and losing one plane and pilot to the Channel.

The next two missions proved uneventful except for the 353rd which had a flight stray on the way home and jumped by a large enemy force. They lost three pilots in this fracas, which prompted Howard to remind us not to relax our mutual support formations even en route home from missions.

On February 10 we took off for an escort mission to Braunschweig. About ten or fifteen minutes inside the enemy coast a single 109 which must have been hanging above us in the layer of intermittent cloud cover bounced us. No one saw him until he had almost reached the outboard flight on a vertical overhead pass. Whoever saw him called for a break for the flight, but it was too late. He sprayed lead all over the flight, though the only plane hit was Lieutenant George Barris's which quietly rolled slowly over into a circling dive and disappeared. I saw the 109 flash by the rear of the squadron in a vertical dive, and rolled to the right into a vertical chase, picking him up at 10,000 feet below as he began to pull out of his dive. I had a little trouble finding him with my bullets because of our high air speeds, but after coordinating a little left rudder with forward stick, the now familiar API strikes blossomed around his wing root and cockpit fuselage area, and the plane yawed wildly to the right skidding and porpoising as if the pilot had lost the stick. I flashed by him, and pulled up in a climbing turn to rejoin the squadron which had continued on course to rendezvous. I assumed from the position of my hits and the sudden wild gyrations of his plane that I had killed the pilot, and as I climbed back to the squadron I wondered whether Barris had been killed, or whether his radio had been disabled. If so, I hoped he had seen me clobber the 109 that had picked him off.

I was approaching the bomber stream now where the group and squadron was already deployed and fighting judging from the RT. I broke into the area looking for friend or foe, but all I could find were the big bombers serenely making their homeward turn amid flak bursts.

I flew patrol around the bombers for forty minutes on their homeward journey hoping to pick up sneak attacks by stray enemy planes, for I could hear the group over the RT engaging the enemy somewhere in the vicinity. However there were no attacks, and when I saw the Channel coastline I collected a couple of stray Mustangs which had gravitated to the bomber stream, and made a beeline for home since my fuel was getting low. After landing I was told that I had missed a nice Donnybrook at rendezvous, while I was chasing the 109. The group had gotten eight "kills," one "probable," and eighteen "damaged." Three planes from the Group had been lost, including Barris. It wasn't long, though, until we got a call canceling one of the losses.

The plane of Captain Glenn Eagleston of the 353rd had been hit, but he'd managed to get it back over England where he bailed out. He told us later that he parachuted down over a division of English Homeguard on maneuvers in an open field. They were so intent on what they were doing that they hadn't noticed Glenn floating down above them. When he got about twenty feet above them he yelled, "Hey!" He thought their startled reaction was funny until he saw they had all spontaneously trained their rifles on him. Then he began yelling, *"AMERICAN, AMERICAN, AMERICAN!"* at the top of his lungs, at the same time trying to get his body ready for the landing shock. It was touch and go for a few moments until an officer came up to him.

On the 11th of February we were scheduled for a bomber escort mission to Frankfurt. Colonel Kenneth R. Martin conducted the briefing that morning, reminding us of certain tactical policies practiced by the Group—

among them the fact that we never turn away from a head-on attack, but either shot the attacker down, or made him turn away. The colonel was soon to prove to us that he himself firmly upheld these principles. It was a normally high overcast day as we took off and set course for rendezvous. After arrival and deployment I was leading my flight in patrol sweeps at three o'clock high parallel to the bomber stream which was entering the bombing run.

Halfway down the sweep, my element leader called out four bogies diving toward the bomber stream at two o'clock level. I spotted them, and though I couldn't identify them, I knew it was very unlikely that any of our own escort would intentionally dive toward the bomber stream. I winged over into an intercepting dive, and instructed the element to take the last two bogies. As we came within identification range I could see that they were ME-109s. Their flight broke into separate elements as the last two planes turned toward us. I ignored them, knowing I was covered by my element, and I led my wingman on to intercept the German leader and wingman who had continued their dive for the bombers. It was clear that we would intercept them long before they came into firing range of the bombers, so I eased the nose of the plane up slightly to acquire a 30-degree lead on the leading 109 with my gunsight pip. As I opened fire, the leader crossed in front of me, evading the converging 50-caliber slugs. But in doing so, he pulled his wingman into the convergent zone of my fire, and it practically obliterated him and his cockpit. One down and one to go. Pulling around with increased pressure on the stick I tailed the leader who had now abandoned any hope of a pass at the bombers in his efforts to escape us. Seeing us coming around for him, the 109 flipped over on his back, and splitessed for cloud cover near the ground. I started over with him, but noticing that the altimeter reading was at 4600 feet, I pulled up and set for climb knowing that I might have led my wingman into a tight squeeze had I followed the Messerschmitt. My wingman must have holed him, for I noticed that as he rolled over he spewed a cloud of thick coolant vapor behind him. Returning to the bombers, we aided those of the screen in intercepting and turning away half-hearted thrusts from stray enemy fighters. We were unable to close combat for the rest of our escort, and when fuel dictated we set course for home.

CHAPTER 4

After the last group Mustang landed that afternoon of the eleventh, results of the mission were as usual made public. The score totaled fourteen enemy aircraft destroyed and ten damaged. We suffered two losses, one of these being Colonel Martin, the Group Commander. According to reports Colonel Martin had carried out his policy regarding head-on attacks to the letter. He had collided with a 109, when neither he nor the German pilot would break off. Miraculously, Martin was thrown clear of the wreckage, and was able to parachute to earth where he was captured by the enemy. He survived his injuries and imprisonment and was returned to us toward the conclusion of the war, but his was a serious loss for the group at this time. Fortunately for the group Jim Howard was immediately placed in command of the group.

The men in the squadron had expected a major or lieutenant colonel to be transferred in to assume the CO position Jim had vacated. To the surprise of us all, it was I who was promoted to the job of squadron commander. I was only a captain, and a newly promoted one at that, and the inherent responsibilities of the new job made me unsure of my own qualifications for the position. I even went so far as to suggest to Howard that I would just as soon remain with the squadron as a flight commander. Howard made it very clear that he "didn't give a damn what I'd just as soon do," pointing out that it was his responsibility to assign positions in the best interest of the squadron, not the individual. It was the finest compliment I ever received, and the only time I was ever reprimanded and commended at the same time.

The three months of continuous combat activity resulted in a 75 percent change-over in command structure for the 354th. The first change came when the original commander of the 353rd Fighter Squadron, Major Owen M. Seaman, lost in the North Sea en route from a mission on December 16, was replaced by Captain Robert L. Priser. Priser was downed over the Brussels area on January 24. He was replaced by Captain Jack T. Bradley who kept the command until near the end of the war. The 355th Fighter Squadron was commanded by Major George R. Bickell, or "Uncle George" as everyone affectionately called him, his command changed later when Howard, considered too valuable to risk in further combat, was involuntarily absorbed into the Ninth Air Force Command. "Uncle George" was then given command of the group, placing Captain Bob Stephens in command of the 355th Fighter Squadron. This was around the 10th of April.

I missed the next four missions as Colonel Howard used the squadron as lead in his new role as group leader. During this period of forced inactivity I missed some good fights, for during these missions the group scored thirty-nine "destroyed," five "probable," and twenty "damaged," losing only three of our planes. Meanwhile,

I got used to my new position as squadron commander, and led a few training missions over England.

My first combat mission as squadron commander was on February 25 to Fürth, and while I didn't get to tangle with the enemy myself, Frank O'Connor celebrated for me by chalking up his fifth kill, and becoming a member of the mythical ranks of "ACES" now beginning to accumulate in the group. I was looking for my eighth kill, but had found lean pickings since my last victory on the eleventh. It was these lean periods that every fighter pilot experienced which whetted our appetite and eagerness for more combat.

February 29, 1944, we flew a mission to Brunswick, and I lost Lieutenant Jim Lane, my first pilot as CO. It was a hard blow for me for Jim had been an old classmate of 42-I. During assembly on the runway at take-off, Lane had parked too long downwind with his engine running thus depriving his radiator of sufficient air cooling, and popped his coolant overflow valve. It was standard procedure to abort the mission and let an alternate take your place when this happened, but Lane had been grounded for some time by the flight surgeon and had only recently regained flying status. He had been impatiently looking forward to this mission, feeling behind the rest of us in opportunities for kills. Ignoring the rule of aborting, he deliberately took off in his regular position. Below 20,000 feet his engine operated normally, but once the Group got to rendezvous altitude at 25,000 feet and the loss of coolant caught up with him overheating the engine and causing it to fail. By the time anyone was aware of his trouble there was nothing we could do to help him as he deadsticked his Mustang down to inevitable capture. It was a tragic and unnecessary loss, for we encountered no enemy opposition on the mission. It was, however, a sad lesson to the squadron on the high cost of negligence.

The 2nd of March we were sent to patrol the area of Beaumont-Hamel, Saint-Andres, Conches, and Evreux, the object being to destroy the Luftwaffe air bases in the area thus preventing interception efforts on scheduled bomber attacks nearby. The mission was executed with no enemy opposition.

On the 3rd we took off on an escort mission to Orainienburg. Flying my wing was a newly arrived young pilot, Lieutenant Bob Davis. Since wingman to the squadron commander was about the best covered position, it was our habit to break new pilots into combat in this slot. I had just deployed the squadron and taken up patrol sweeps with Red flight when I caught sight of four ME-109s diving for the bombers at one o'clock high. Calling in the bandits to my flight, I canted over in a dive trying to intercept before they reached the bombers, but the distance between us was too great for me to make it in time. Determined to hit the Germans and break them up, I increased my diving angle, and prepared to go through the edge of the bomber formation in chase of the Messerschmitts. This was always dangerous, because the bombers couldn't be expected to tell the difference between us and the Jerries, and would no doubt throw lead at us too, but I counted on their preoccupation with the Germans ahead of us to reduce their attention on us.

Meanwhile, I was unaware that another ME-109, chased by a Mustang, had inadvertently crossed through our diving path, colliding with Lieutenant Davis and had created an explosion which screened me from the sight of my following element led by Lieutenant Lamb. Lamb could only conclude that both Davis and I had exploded, and pulled up and away to avoid the debris, hence losing me. Continuing my dive through the bombers oblivious of the tragic collision behind me, I caught the 109 flight at 8000 feet. I fired on the last craft in the formation, causing him to burst into flame and fall out of formation. The others seeing me for the first time broke apart in three different directions. Still believing my flight to be with me, I called Lamb to take the two running to the right, so I could get the others. Just above deck level, both the Messerschmitt and I leveled off at high speed and I glanced around to discover with a shock that I was all alone, my flight nowhere to be seen. Turning back to the 109 I planned to make a quick hit and get back upstairs to find friendly company. But before I could line up my sights I heard someone yelling over the RT "*Break left!*" I didn't pause to ask stupid questions, but hauled the stick back into my gut, and left the fleeing 109 in a screaming high "g" turn. I looked up to the rear in time to see another 109 flash by with a Mustang hot on his tail. Completing my turn, I joined the other Mustang, Captain Jack Bradley, CO of the 353rd. We cruised around a while looking for fights, then climbed back to the bomber area where we collected a few of our respective dispersed squadrons, and headed back to base. At base I learned of the accidental collision between Lieutenant Davis and the 109. In fact I had been listed as MIA until I landed, as Lamb had thought both Davis and I had been involved in the mid-air collision. The Group posted two kills that day, one of them being the 109 I had caught below the bombers. Davis was our sole loss, the only wingman I ever lost on a combat mission.

On March 4 the Group flew an area support mission in the Berlin area which I missed since Colonel Howard had borrowed my squadron again for the group lead. They destroyed one German, but lost Lieutenant Robert Silva and Edward Fox of the 353rd east of Berlin.

Two days later we were again briefed for a mission to Berlin, but this time we were to give penetration and withdrawal support to the heavies. Colonel George Bickell led the group with the 355th. Arriving at rendezvous we found the weather topped out at 27,000 feet, and the bombers down in it at 25,000. Just short of Berlin the bombers received a mission abort signal, and the lead division made a 180-degree turn in the soup. From our position at 30,000 feet we could see huge clouds of black smoke come boiling up out of the clouds, indicating a collision. A few minutes later we came to a break in the weather which extended to the ground. No bomber stream emerged from the clouds, and we soon deduced that they had been recalled. As we flew on in group formation we could see fifteen to thirty con trails at one o'clock high, which were identified as bandits, ME-109s. Bickell started a turn to the right as they passed over us, and this threw us to the rear of the group as we crossed over in the turn, exposing my squadron's tails to the Messerschmitts overhead. The whole group of Germans came at us in a diving attack.

I ordered the squadron to drop tanks and break to the right, and started to haul in on the stick. At this moment my engine quit cold! My blood chilled as I slumped down in the cockpit to grab my fuel switch, knowing instantly that I had forgotten to switch from drop tanks to internal before releasing. I was flying a P-51B with a Malcolm bubble canopy modification which frosted irregularly at the right-hand lower canopy edge from coolant vapor thrown from the engine at high altitude. When Lamb saw me slump down in the cockpit, and what he thought was a jagged hole in the canopy as my plane lost speed and staggered away from him, he thought I had been hit by cannon fire, and he picking up my wingman, continued the break away from me. After four or five seconds the engine restarted, and I nosed down to gain flying speed again, and looked to the rear—straight into the guns of four 109s coming down fast on my tail! I was cold meat! At minimum flying speed with no flight to help, I couldn't think of what to do. Some subconscious instinct must have moved my hand to the flap lever handle. As the flaps hit the slipstream, the Mustang almost hung in mid-air, full power keeping it from spinning. The 109s flashed by me without scoring a hit from their firing guns. As they passed I pulled up the flaps, and dove after them increasing my speed, and chances to live. But one of the 109s used my own trick and slid high in a skid killing his speed, and keeping me at a disadvantage as I went for his wingman. The other two splitessed for the deck as they overshot me. Trying to place the pip on the 109 in front of me, and at the same time keep track of the smart cookie almost abreast of me now required some real fast thinking. I knew to have any chance at all I had to get rid of them both in a hurry, and concentrating on the one in front of me, hit him with a long hard burst of 50s from dead astern. He took a flash of hits about the cockpit and at the wing root, which exploded his ammo and snapped off his left wing. The canopy and pilot followed the wing in short order. Jerking my head around, I found the other 109 high behind me making another diving pass. I had again lost speed because of the long gun burst at high altitude, and I had a little trouble turning to the left to get out of the path of the oncoming Messerschmitt. As he saw me turning, he swung high again and turned in behind me, again setting up for a firing pass. With his speed advantage the 109 was soon in range, and in desperation I prepared to skid violently down to the left as soon as I saw his guns start blinking. The 109 was in perfect range, and yet he didn't fire. As I waited for the sight of those blinking muzzle flashes the suspense was terrific. He seemed to fall back a little, and hesitantly bob his left wing slightly as if he were undecided about winging over into a dive. Puzzled, I took a quick glance around, and saw the most beautiful sight in the world. Two Mustangs were rushing toward me from eleven o'clock high. No wonder the 109 was hanging back! I started a turn to the left hoping to suck the German after me in order to give the two Mustangs a better shot at him, but he was no fool. Over and down he went making tracks for the Fatherland. I was almost overcome with relief, and called the Mustangs which were now coming alongside me, the leader wagging his wings for join up. The leader was Bob Goodnight, my old flying buddy. When he discovered who I was he laughed and told me he'd let me fly along under his protection. I called back that I wasn't proud, and that I'd be happy to accept. That was the closest that I ever came, and the closest I ever want to come, to being shot down. I still get chills when I remember looking into those gun barrels. Returning to base we found that the group had exacted eight scalps from the German 109s that had attacked us. We had lost one pilot from the 353rd, a Lieutenant Ridley Donnell.

A return visit to Berlin was scheduled on the 8th, and this time the bombers made it. We ran into little opposition, but O'Connor found a couple of overly curious 109s poking around the outskirts of the bomber stream, and promptly rewarded their curiosity by providing them two brilliantly burning funeral pyres. Lieutenant Carl Frantz of the 353rd flamed a FW-190 that ventured too close to the bombers. The rest of us had to be content with chasing stray enemy aircraft who were reluctant to close, and all we got were strikes at long range with doubtful results.

En route back to the Channel I found a B-17 struggling along with two feathered props, and I contacted him on "B" (Baker) channel to tell him my flight would stay with him until he made it to mid-Channel. I had the flight switch to "B" channel for tactical control so we could use the extra eyes in the bomber crew, and positioned the flight in separate element patrol orbits above the crippled bomber. We guided him around congested areas and airfields, and ran hit and run strafing passes on any flak sites that appeared in our path. In what seemed like no time at all, we slid past the Dutch coastline out to sea much to our relief, for we were beginning to run low on fuel. Finally after a last clearing orbit, and assurances from the bomber pilot that he could make England, we lined the flight out to the southwest, homing on radio voice steer signals from Boxsted. This mission resulted in three victories and no losses.

On March 16 we were briefed for penetration and

general area support patrol at Augsburg. I was looking for my tenth victory, but it seemed like the Jerries had let up in their efforts at interception lately, and I took off without expecting much action. But as the old Indian fighter used to say, "When you least expect them the critters show up." On this mission the group and squadrons broke up into flights for general saturation patrol sweeps directly to the bomber stream. I took my flight straight for the bombers, thinking this would be the most productive hunting ground. My hunch paid off. As we drove up to the stream of bombers I noticed a sun glint at one o'clock high. Squinting into the glare, I could see the silhouettes of four 109s tilted in a dive for the stream. Calling to my flight to pick their counterparts for individual attack I dropped into a dive of interception. Halfway the Germans caught sight of us, for they changed course, using the bombers as a screen instead of continuing their attack. I guess they were counting on our reluctance to charge through bomber formations, but what they didn't know was how eager I was to get a crack at my tenth victory.

As the Messerschmitts dove behind the other side, I chose the least crowded area and flashed through the stream. I lost my flightmates, who had more sense than I did, and who pulled up and away from the stream as I penetrated it. Emerging from the cluster of bombers, who evidently recognized me as one of their own, I found two 109s below me running to the southeast. They saw me as I bounced them, and pulled into a tight right turn. Following them, I fired a wide arching burst of tracers which ended in a fiery rain just in front of the leader. To my complete astonishment the pilot, seeing the hail of tracer fire immediately in front of him, jettisoned his canopy and bailed out. Recovering from my surprise, I looked for the other 109, which had rolled out of the turn and was diving for a low cloud bank. Rolling after him, I had just gotten range when he entered the cloud bank. I set up an orbit just above the clouds, and took pot shots as he emerged every few seconds for observation. We played hide and seek for a few minutes until I remembered I was alone at a mere 8000 feet over his own territory where German aid could reach him if I gave him enough time to direct them. Throwing a parting burst of 50s where I thought he might be, I pulled up in a climbing turn and headed back to the bomber stream area. A few seconds later I saw ahead of me the parachuting pilot of the 109 I had shot (scared) down a few minutes before. Pointing the plane at him, I flipped the gun switch to "camera only" to get a picture, but the thought crossed my mind that this circuit had been known to foul up and fire the guns, so, I restrained my desire to get a confirming picture of my victim. Instead I turned aside, passing within thirty feet of him. I suppose when he saw me point straight at him, he fully expected to be gunned down, for he had drawn himself up and crossed his arms in front of his face as if to ward off the bullets, and when he saw me turn aside without firing, and waggling my wings as I passed he started waving his arms and grinning like a Cheshire cat. I thought as I climbed that since he had provided me with my tenth victory, he deserved a break. I just hoped he'd live to spread the word that Americans didn't shoot helpless pilots in parachutes. Maybe the Germans would follow suit.

Returning to the bomber area I prowled around looking for more stray Germans, but found none. So, picking up a couple of wandering Mustangs I set course for homebase. En route home Captain Verlin Chambers and Lieutenant Floyd Brandt attacked a strange-looking object which they described as an HE-111 with a ME-109 mounted on its back. The group had collected twelve victories and three damaged enemy aircraft that day, losing one Mustang flown by T/Sergeant Donald Dempsey of the 353rd. Dempsey had been one of five flying T/Sergeants assigned to the group recently—an unusual rank for pilots which was soon eliminated. It was basically unfair to have them fly combat missions in which they were expected to assume all the responsibilities of officers without having the same status on the ground. I had two of these boys assigned to me—a T/Sergeant Aney and a T/Sergeant John Ferguson, and I kept the lines between group and squadron hot with persistent requests for their promotion to second lieutenant, or at least to the warrant commission of flight officer. Though I disliked having them fly combat missions I was obliged to let them fly some because of the need for pilots.

The group flew seven more missions during the month of March accumulating thirteen more victories and eight losses. Two of these were from my squadron—T/Sergeant Aney and Lieutenant Theodore Ditewig, who were lost on a mission that I hadn't flown. The only mission I participated in during this period was as top cover for a dive bombing mission over Creil, France, in which we experienced no opposition or losses. We now began to get more and more missions involving dive bombing and strafing, and this increase was our first hint that per-

11. My first P-51, "Short-Fuse Sallee," at Boxted, England in early 1944.

12. Lt. Mailon Gillis.

13. Lt. George Hall.

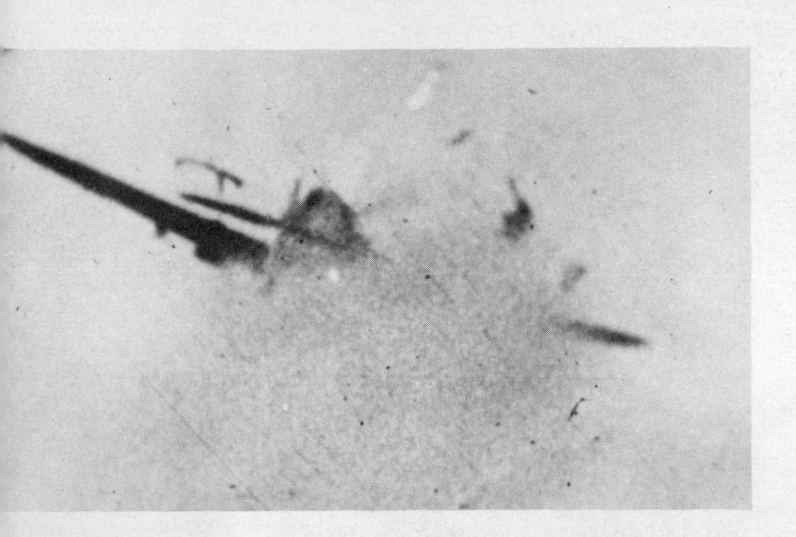

14. This Me-109G, shot down on January 11, 1944, was my third confirmed victory.

15. Leading my squadron back to base in echelon formation for peel-off prior to landing.

16. Men of the 356th outside the ready hut at Boxted.

17. I loaned my fighter to F/O Ferguson and he nosed it up after landing.

18. Jack Bradley, 15 victories, 353rd F.S.

19. Bob Stephens, 13 victories, 355th F.S.

20. Bob Stephens' P-51D, "Killer."

haps the long-awaited invasion of the Continent was being prepared.

It was about this time that I had a very poignant experience with one of our squadron crew chiefs. Our ground crews were invariably the last to quit work and the first to start every day. They worked without urging long into the wet, cold, bleak nights repairing battle damage, and tuning the Mustangs for peak performance every day. It was a matter of personal pride that they provide their pilots with the best planes that ever took off to battle the Luftwaffe. They would polish the wings of a plane to a high gloss in an effort to reduce air friction, adding an extra five to ten miles per hour to its air speed. These men worked constantly on the problem of gun stoppage caused by the angle mount of the 50-caliber guns in the wings of the B model, and had instituted a squadron modification which was eventually adopted by all Mustangs in the ETO. It involved mounting booster feed motors along the ammo chutes to overcome the "G" forces encountered in dive pullouts and hard turns. Having worked late into the night, they would rise early in the morning to check the engines, being sure they were warmed up before take-off time. This enthusiasm generated a feeling of warm regard between the pilots and their ground crews.

One day S/Sergeant Volie P. Miller, a crew chief, requested permission to speak to me. I was astonished at his request to be relieved from the duties of crew chief, the position being one of the most coveted in the noncommissioned ranks. Miller had a fine record as a top crew chief, and I could see when I asked the reason for his unusual request that a condition of deep emotion threatened to break up his composure. Tears were appearing in his eyes in spite of his effort to contain himself. With mounting concern over the sergeant's unusual emotional condition I asked him to sit down and tell me what was bothering him. It developed he was worried about the squadron's combat losses. Although our squadron had lowest total losses in the Group, we had lost three or four during the past four months, and by some quirk of fate Sergeant Miller had been crew chief to two of the pilots. He had led himself to believe that he was to blame for the losses. I had a very hard time convincing him that mechanical failure of the planes seldom, if ever, caused a combat loss. I pointed out that our squadron record of aborts was almost infinitesimal in relation to the number of sorties we had flown, and emphasized that our ground crews were doing a superior job maintaining the aircraft for the pilots. Every pilot in the squadron would have been quick to support my opinion. I was finally able to convince Sergeant Miller that he was in no way responsible for the combat loss of his pilots. It was an emotionally exhausting experience for both of us and one I'll remember for the rest of my life, for it exemplifies the unique brotherly bonds which can be established between each crew chief and his pilot. I know I would have fought tooth and nail to avoid losing my own crew chief, T/Sergeant Clint Thompson of Hatfield, Missouri, who served with me throughout the war. Tommy celebrated every victory we scored as if they were his own, which, in a way, they were. For without his unstinting cooperation and long hours of work under the most trying conditions, I could never have been so successful. In all of my ninety-seven missions, I aborted only one, and that was caused by an undetectable particle in a hydraulic line on an over-age Mustang which prevented me from raising my landing gear.

March ended our fourth month of combat, and the group had flown forty-five combat missions, had shot down 159 Germans, and lost forty-five men and forty-seven planes. Our squadron had accounted for about a third of the victories, and lost only four pilots in combat, a record we were justly proud of. We were determined to maintain this trend and high score. The 356th Squadron ultimately destroyed 298 German aircraft losing only twenty-two pilots in combat and training accidents—a kill/loss ratio of better than 13/1. As far as I know this is the finest record ever achieved by an Air Force squadron in continual combat for over an eighteen-month period, and I am understandably proud to have been with such an outstanding group of men.

During our early days of combat we had become quickly accustomed to the fact that our long range escort missions called for up to five hours of sitting in the cramped cockpit of the Mustang fighters. The discomfort we experienced led us to adopt as our squadron insignia a cavorting Red Ass.

We started our fifth month of combat on a mission of penetration support for the bombers to Ludwigshafen. Though I encountered no enemy, one of the group did, shooting down two and damaging two more. All our men returned unscathed.

Four days later, on April 5, we took off on a fighter sweep of Luftwaffe airfields in Châteauroux, Conches, Chartres, and Bourges. At a point central to the targets the group separated, and I led my squadron to hit Bourges.

Twenty miles from target I instructed Green flight to fly over Bourges at 10,000 feet as top cover, and deployed Red, White, and Blue flights on courses at deck level so they could hit from three different directions at one-minute intervals. I hit the field first with Red flight, and caught a landing ME-410, hitting him on the landing roll and causing him to burst into flames leaving a trail of debris down the runway. Banking around after my first pass, I dived on a ME-110 being serviced on a hardstand, starting a raging fire beneath him as my incendiaries and those of my wingman ignited the gasoline spilling from his tanks. Pulling up again, I rolled over and down on another twin-engined craft poised at the edge of the field with props revving for take-off. The burst from my 50s chewed into him at perfect range, and he blew up. Calling the squadron, I told everyone to climb to 15,000 feet and rendezvous ten miles northwest of Bourges. The German's surprise had worn off, and flak reaction was coming hot and heavy. Everyone except Goodnight got away safe. He had attempted one last pass on a camouflaged fighter at the edge of the airfield. As he completed the pass, he was hit with a 20-mm right below his cockpit. Goodnight called out over the RT that his plane was hit, but he thought he could still fly it, so I told him to come on home with us, and we'd get it fixed for him when we landed. With Bob fuming over the RT about "hardhearted squadron commanders" we made our way home, unhindered by the Germans except for an occasional heavy flak burst. Back at base we found one of the other squadrons wasn't so lucky and had lost a fighter and pilot to flak while strafing. But the group had destroyed six enemy aircraft, with one probable and four damaged. We were all convinced of one thing: that was that it was a lot more difficult to attack German aircraft on the ground than in a nice uncomplicated air fight.

CHAPTER 5

I celebrated my twenty-fourth birthday on April 8 by flying a penetration-support mission for the heavy bombers to Brunswick, Germany. After rendezvous and deployment my flight tangled with four diving ME-109s, and in the resultant scramble we were all separated. I caught my prey after a long twisting dive toward the ground, and flamed him into a falling torch. Starting my pull-out, I discovered another ME-109 flying along at treetop level. I nosed over into a shallow dive to catch him. He was going full out, and we twisted and turned for ten minutes as I attempted to shoot him down first at long range, and then at shorter range in sharp turns with our wingtips almost brushing the treetops. My guns had overheated and burned away their accuracy because of the long bursts I was using. Tracers were corkscrewing all over the place, and I could have used a flyswatter more effectively. Finally the German plane bobbed low and I flew as close as I could get behind him. As he reached a line of trees at the far end of a cleared field I pulled back and sprayed a wild bunch of tracers which went just over his canopy. Evidently, as he popped up over the hedgerow he saw the streaks of the tracers passing overhead and instinctively pushed forward on the stick to duck under them. Instantly his 109 caught the tall trees, and crashed in a long slash of boiling smoke.

Chandelling up to a west heading, I stayed near the deck to look around, and after a couple of minutes I saw a large clear area ahead in which sat an HE-111 parked for service. I nosed down and tripped a hail of still erratic bullets. I saw a few API strikes on the Henkel, and had the satisfaction at least of knowing I had left a few holes in the blasted thing. With my guns practically useless for accurate shooting and being still 400 miles deep inside Germany I decided I needed some friendly company but fast. I started climbing for the bombers at top speed.

Halfway out of enemy territory I caught up with the bombers on the homeward leg, but I couldn't find any of our friendly fighters. It looked as if it were up to me to escort the entire stream home—or rather I reconciled myself to being escorted home by them. I called the bombers on "B" channel, identified myself as a Mustang, and throttled back to assume patrol station a thousand feet above them. A couple of lone ME-109s started passes at different times, but to my relief they splitessed to the deck when they saw my Mustang bluff a countering pass. The nearest bomber pilots made witty remarks over "B" channel about the brave Mustang pilot protecting their honor, but their jocularity died when I informed them their brave Mustang pilot had no guns and was just bluffing. We made it to the Channel, however, where I rocked my wings at the bombers and dived away toward homebase.

Upon landing I discovered that I hadn't been the only

one busy that afternoon. The group had been embroiled in a raging aerial battle, and had shot down twenty-one Germans with one probable and sixteen damaged. Four of our planes and pilots failed to return, but there was some small comfort in learning that none of them were my boys.

On April 11 we were briefed for a penetration and target support mission to the Cottbus and Sarou area near the Polish border. This was going to be a tail-numbing flight of more than five hours. I had had new machine-gun barrels installed after my last mission, and I was eager to try them on for size. We took off, assembled, and flew for what felt like hours before rendezvousing with the bombers and deploying into a protective screen.

After a few minutes of patrol sweeps I saw three bogies diving through the bomber stream a mile or two down the line. I called out their location to my flight and nosed over in a dive to catch them below the bombers. Instead of pulling up for another pass these birds kept right on diving, and turned for an airfield below. Spotting the airfield I smiled in anticipation, and throttled back to keep from overrunning my quarry, who evidently supposed they had made it safely back to the coop. I delayed our attack to allow the unsuspecting Germans time to spread out on the downwind leg of their landing pattern. There's nothing a pilot fears so much as being caught in the pattern with his wheels down, and I figured that if we didn't get them with our guns we'd *scare* them to death.

Picking the second plane in the pattern, I dropped down with guns firing. He promptly flipped over on his back at 500 feet, and crashed into the ground. I slewed the Mustang into a left-hand turn, and slid high, looking for the first plane in the landing pattern who was now on his final approach. Positioning myself directly behind him, I hit him hard with bursts around his cockpit. He never flared out of his glide, but simply flew the 109 into the ground where it exploded.

Looking out over the airfield I could see no flak, so I made a pass at a large twin-engined craft parked immediately ahead, and scored a cluster of strikes over its wings and fuselage. By now I could see ground fire floating up. I told my flight to hug the deck, and we escaped from the area without a scratch. We returned to base without further contact with the enemy.

I led my squadron with the group on April 12 for a target-penetration to Leipzig. German activity was reported in the area, but my flight had no luck closing with the enemy. The fighters we sighted turned out to be stray Mustangs or bashful bogies which turned and ran at our first move of interception. After thirty or forty minutes of playing this kind of hare and hound, we drifted down to the homeward-turn point of the bomber stream. Swinging south of the westward-bound bombers we were startled to find a lone B-17 struggling on a descending course to the southwest. It was obviously making for Switzerland. We recently had been given unofficial orders that any aircraft found on a course to Switzerland, not in trouble, were to be intercepted, and forced to resume a heading for England. As pilots we were skeptical of this order because we knew there were types of emergencies not perceivable to another airplane, and radio contact with a single bomber was always a hit-or-miss affair.

More from curiosity than anything else I took the flight down to the bomber in a wide descending turn. Inspecting the big bird as we circled, I found that two of its props were feathered, and one of the remaining engines was throwing smoke. This poor devil was in real trouble, and was trying desperately to save his crew from capture by going to Switzerland. Impressed by the pilot's heroic effort I determined to give what little aid and moral support I could by escorting him to the Swiss line. I couldn't raise him on "B" channel, but pulling away from the flight I slowed down to fly formation with him momentarily, and saw two or three airmen crowded up to a waist gun opening waving and gesticulating in vigorous welcome. When the pilot could see me I pointed southwest toward Switzerland, nodded my head affirmative, and gave him the "thumbs up" sign. The pilot smiled broadly, and waved his thanks. My flight and I assumed a circling orbit above the bomber to watch for threats. During the next thirty minutes several curious single bogies nosed in our direction but made no attack upon seeing us.

Finally, as the bomber crossed over Lake Constance into Switzerland, we saw two ME-109s approaching rapidly from the Swiss side, but something indefinable made me hold my fire. We found that they were Swiss fighters come to convoy the disabled bomber to internment landing in Switzerland. Rocking our wings goodbye to the bomber crew we headed for home at an accelerated pace. Although we hadn't shot down any Germans, the experience we had been privileged to participate in gave our morale a great lift.

Back at Boxsted we learned that it had been a fairly

quiet mission for everyone. Someone in the group had caught a stray German to make the day's bag one enemy destroyed, with no losses. This brought the Group record to 208 enemy aircraft destroyed with 33 probables and 147 damaged.

On the 13th of April the group flew a mission to Schweinfurt which I did not join, in order to rotate the squadron lead with one of my experienced officers. In the target area the Group engaged German aircraft and a large scale aerial battle ensued. Upon their return we found they had added fourteen German aircraft destroyed with one probable and eight damaged to the group record of claims.

But the day was marred for the 356th when we learned that two of our fighters were missing. The downed pilots were Lieutenant "Stud" George Hall and Lieutenant Robert Planck. Old Stud had been in our original cadre of pilots in the 356th, and his loss was especially hard for the old-timers among us to take. He had been a dependable fighter pilot, and had contributed much to the aggressive atmosphere and spirit of the squadron. It was reported that while going down over Germany Stud was reeling off a list of debts owed to friends before bailing out. Whether true or not, it was just the kind of stunt Stud would have pulled in the face of danger and death.

We had been alerted by Ninth Air Force that we were to move our base of operations from Boxsted to an advanced landing strip in Kent about ten miles southeast of Maidstone, England. Ground preparations had been in progress for some time, but we were expected to continue our participation in aerial missions uninterruptedly during the move. Therefore, on the 15th of April, we prepared for an extended fighter sweep over northern Germany. About half of the fighter group would work and go on the mission, and the other half was involved in transferring equipment and personnel to our new base, Station 410, at Maidstone.

The mission of the 15th was the first of three consecutive missions to be led by the three squadron commanders in turn, to prepare them for availability as group leaders in the future, and this particular mission was being led by Captain Jack Bradley, commanding officer of the 353rd. Absolutely lousy weather was forecast for the entire mission, and for once the weatherman was 100 percent correct. We took off and droned on and on in these conditions tense on the edge of our seats. To further aggravate matters some clown in one of the squadrons had his "throttle transmitter button" stuck down, and was singing a terrible rendition of "Mairzy Doats" over the Group frequency, effectively nullifying all communications. I hung onto Jack's 353rd Squadron with my 356th in formation watching fearfully lest the changing weather led to a chain reaction of fighters lunging every which way. We could all remember watching the holocaust when the bombers collided in the soup over Berlin. By the time our elapsed time indicated we should be near the target every pilot had become as nervous as a "whore in church."

At this particular time a thick fog bank which extended to the ground from above 20,000 feet abruptly swallowed the 353rd and 355th Squadrons. Within a second or two our "opera singer" went off the air with jarring suddenness. Without reference to the lead squadron I was flying on instruments for all practical purposes, and I grabbed a glance down to the right where I could faintly see a coastline running east and west. Gently easing the squadron around in a wide turning dive I made for this welcome reference point of terra firma. At 2000 feet we came out of the overcast over a bleak expanse of water. Checking the coastline against my map I discovered we were over the Baltic Sea off Rostock, Germany, which was our original target area.

I felt like a Little League pitcher suddenly thrust onto the mound in Yankee Stadium. We had the whole target area to ourselves, but there was not enough visibility to pick out targets, and hardly even enough to keep the squadron together. I decided that it was more important to get my squadron home intact, if possible, than to shoot haphazardly at what would turn out probably to be insignificant targets. I called the squadron, and told them to forget it. We were going home.

I started wending my way through the fog bank toward the west, planning to cross the Kiel Peninsula and pick up the Frisian Islands from where I could set course for England. I wanted desperately to keep the squadron together, for I could imagine the losses if I released sixteen fighters in this soup to roam at random all over northern Germany. My great fear was of inadvertently stumbling over a concentration of flak positions who could detect us in the air much more easily than we could see them. But luck was with us and this threat never materialized. Finding the Frisian Islands we flew down their length to the Wadden Zee and then set course for England. I dropped to 100 feet above the North Sea where I found the visibility was slightly better, and I told the squadron to fly "stepped up" formation above me so that I would be the aircraft closest to the water's surface. Time moves slowly while flying in restricted visibility, and it seemed as if we were flying for hours getting nowhere. I had begun worrying about making landfall when all visibility was lost for a fraction of a second as I flashed through the smoke trail of a northbound steamer. That instant of lost visibility unnerved me, but my fear changed to soaring relief as I saw the coastal steamer, and I looked ahead to see the coast of England looming up.

Coming over the coast I recognized the huge emergency landing strip between Lowestoft and Leiston, which located our base at Boxsted about twenty-five miles to the southwest. I put the full squadron in echeloned flights, and made a pass over the field. We were the first ones back, and the only squadron to return intact as a unit. The other squadrons landed all over Britain having been hopelessly split up in the vicious fog. Miraculously the group sustained no losses, and eventually all our wandering planes returned.

CHAPTER 6

By the 17th of April we had completed our move to Maidstone, and we flew our planes to the new air strip and a "strip" it was! Its surface was made of the new metal interlocking strips which were laid down over quickly compacted earth. These strips were fine for normal operations, but were deadly when wet. If you applied too much power suddenly on the wet metal during taxiing and take-off the torque force of the prop could neatly swing you 90 degrees away from your intended path. We also exchanged our comfortable Nissen huts for foxholes until squadron tents were set up. More than ever now it was evident we were being groomed for things to come, for the long-awaited Invasion, we hoped.

It wasn't long, however, before we had officer and enlisted clubs operating in circus tents and life was made bearable again.

On the 18th of April it fell my lot to lead the assembled Group. Checking in at Group Operations, I found we were scheduled to provide withdrawal support for the heavies from Rathenow and Brandenburg just west of Berlin. After getting my intelligence and weather data I worked out the rendezvous course for the Group with the Group Operations officer, and went to briefing.

We took off from Maidstone, and I led the Group over the Canterbury barrage balloons. The weather was fairly decent ahead of us, but I could see a lot of weather from frontal action just to the north of us where we should normally see the bomber stream lined out on its return from target. Rendezvous time arrived but there was no bomber stream in sight. Checking my ground references I knew I was in the right area, and the only possible explanation was that the bombers were in or behind the clouds to the north of us. I deployed the Group, sending one squadron over the weather to see if the bombers were on the other side, leaving one squadron in rendezvous position in case bombers emerged on this side, then took my lead squadron on to target area in case the bombers were still at target behind schedule. I never did find out what the full story of the bombers was, because each squadron found a few of them to escort home. The stream must have been scattered in the weather, for we found them all over Germany and behind every cloud bank. This, fortunately was one of the Luftwaffe's quiet days. We located our bombers where ever we could find them and shepherded them home without interference. Eventually everyone came home without claims or loss.

Captain Bob Stephens, CO of the 355th Squadron, took his turn at the group lead on April 19. It was to be a dive-bombing mission against rail installations at Namur, France. We all were to carry two 500-pound bombs, one under each wing where we normally carried drop tanks of extra fuel. Bob headed us south, across the Channel to make landfall over Dieppe, and then on to our target.

We hadn't been over the Channel more than three minutes when I got a call from my wingman telling me that the fins of my 500-pounders had fallen off, and the bombs appeared to be smoking badly. I called Captain O'Connor, leader of the White flight, and told him to take the lead.

Telling my wingman to stay with the mission I peeled out of the formation and away to be alone over the Channel in case the bombs blew in mid-air. As I watched the group formation recede into the distance leaving me with my two spooky bombs, I began to get a mighty lonely feeling. For some reason this brought to mind those wartime signs I used to see back in the States: IS THIS TRIP REALLY NECESSARY? Snapping back to the present, I realized the bombs hadn't gone off as yet—which meant perhaps they wouldn't at all. In fact, the more I thought of it the less likely it seemed, for from what I knew about bombs I realized they had to fall free for several hundred feet before they were even armed. Finally convincing myself that they were relatively harmless while still in the racks, I pondered what to do with the damned things. It was standard procedure in such cases as mine to dump them in the Channel; but it galled me to throw them away without doing damage to the Germans. I could see Boulogne on the French coast not five miles away, and it seemed a shame to waste my bombs with targets so near.

Then I had an inspiration! Abbeville, the famous old aerodrome of Baron Von Richthofen, and presently, so it was rumored, the lair of Goering's "yellow nosed bandits" was no more than a few minutes away, and here I had a perfect opportunity to pay them a personal visit. As the English say, "Wizard show!"

It took me only a short time to find the beautifully laid-out Abbeville complex, and it seems I caught them busy in a working day. At 10,000 feet I rolled over into a vertical dive, and began working over the entire field with my 50-caliber machine guns. At 3000 feet I had picked the largest cluster of buildings for a bomb release. Dropping the bombs, I pulled out low, and started a shallow climb toward the Channel. With a great shock I saw off to the right of the field the largest, meanest-looking heavy gun emplacement I had ever seen. The whole German Army was running for those guns, and about forty light gun positions dotted around the field. I had always been taught that if you saw you were going to get hit, it was better nine times out of ten to get the first lick in.

Praying that this wouldn't be that "tenth time" I rolled into a strafing dive on the emplacement, feeling much like a mosquito going after an elephant. I started spraying lead at long range all over the area. Soon a flurry of tracers that seemed as big as baseballs were crisscrossing all around me in return fire. But I must have at least shaken up the gun crews a bit, for I didn't receive a scratch and was soon hugging the deck going wide open to the northwest. After putting three or four miles between me and the emplacement I began an erratic climb for altitude and home.

After landing I was in high spirits; I leaped down from my fighter wing to see the Group Commander, Lieutenant Colonel "Uncle" George Bickell who stood waiting for me. I thought it unusually nice of him to greet me personally upon my return. What he had come for, however, was to chew me out. It seems the English had complained about the unscheduled and unauthorized combat operation carried out by a crazy American against a German airfield near the coast of France. It seems it just wasn't "in the form" (whatever *that* meant), and it "wouldn't do!" I was worried until I saw that "Uncle" George was laughing. I explained the cause of the unscheduled attack, and told him to explain it away as due to my lousy navigation.

Two days later the three squadron commanders received their promotions to major, and "Uncle" George got his eagles as full colonel. Now I was Major Turner, but I didn't enjoy the lift in rank as much as I had expected. There were many good fighter pilots such as Frank O'Connor, Bob Goodnight, Max Lamb and others that deserved the promotion as much or perhaps even more than I did; but I've got to admit I wasn't too unhappy to accept the promotion.

On April 23 the Group flew two missions, a dive-bombing sortie over Namur again, and a fighter sweep in the Hannover area. I flew the dive-bombing mission. I suppose Command was taking no chances on another private war on Abbeville, for this time I was assigned the top cover protection of the dive-bombers. Neither mission produced any contact with enemy aircraft, nor did we lose any men.

Two days later we took off with great expectations for an extended fighter sweep in the Mannheim area, and as we deployed, the action developed quickly to everyone's satisfaction—except mine. Everyone, myself excepted, found German fighters lurking behind every cloud. I could hear fights raging all around me, but I couldn't even find a kite.

It was a very frustrating afternoon; the only excitement

for my flight came as I led them home. We were on course for southern England, and flying over a thick cloud layer which prevented us from seeing check points on the ground. In our progress we unwittingly flew directly over the Saar Basin normally avoided by all Allied aircraft because of the tremendous concentration of heavy flak there to protect the region's vital steel industry. Our first hint that we had goofed came from a string of flak bursts expertly placed to each side and in front of the flight, looking all the world like runway markers inviting us to land. Needless to say we refused, and abruptly commenced desperate formation acrobatics. There were literally hundreds of 88s and 105s firing at us as the sky turned black with menacing oily smoke. I could have sworn the guns below were following each of us in our every move.

After what seemed to be a half hour trying to outguess the tenacious gun crews we finally flew out of range, toward homebase. Exhausted we made our way to Maidstone, and landed. It seems that we had done most of the hard work, while the rest of the group reaped the harvest. They had destroyed eighteen German aircraft with five probable and thirty-one damaged. The cost of this big mission was two planes and pilots. Lieutenant E. R. Carr was missing in action, and Lieutenant William Simmons was known to have bailed out.

Our next mission on the 26th of April provided me with one of the biggest thrills of my flying career. We went on a mission to Brunswick, and after penetrating enemy territory for some thirty minutes an element in one of my squadron flights reported problems with their drop tank fuel. I knew we would need all the fuel we had on this mission, so I instructed them to abort the mission and return to base together. The element—Lieutenant Mailon Gillis and Lieutenant Leonard Jackson—acknowledged my transmission, and peeled out of the squadron. The Group proceeded flying northeast expecting to see the bomber stream and target area of Brunswick within the hour. But the longer we flew the more uncomfortable we all became. The terrain below was unfamiliar, and rendezvous with the bombers was long overdue. An uneasiness gradually settled over the Group as we came to the slow realization that we were, in fact, lost somewhere in the middle of Europe.

When it finally became apparent that we could not find the bombers, the Group leader released the squadrons for individual return to base. I started to do some fast figuring trying to grasp what had gone wrong. I heard the other squadrons dispersing into individual flights, but I decided to keep the 356th intact in case we had a chance to bounce some Germans; moreover, as squadron commander I felt responsible for all my planes, and not merely for my own flight. I reasoned that the only factor explaining our present position was a strong north wind causing us to have drifted far south of course. I set a heading out to the northwest rather than the normal westerly course for return. After flying this course for two hours, instead of making the coastline near the Hague as anticipated, we recognized Calais beneath us. From Calais it was just a stone's throw to base, but it meant we were some 200 miles south of our scheduled position: we had an unpredicted wind from the north of monumental proportions!

Landing the squadron I found Group Command concerned over no less than five missing planes. We received a report that there were winds 100 mph greater than those predicted over the Continent today. Since no combat had been reported, it was feared that the five planes had been lost somewhere in southern France as they tried to fly back to England. Worst yet, two of the missing planes were my fliers, Gillis and Jackson. I immediately asked for permission to take a single Mustang south in an effort somehow to reach them and lead them home.

Without waiting for an answer I ordered my Mustang refueled, and took off for the area of Le Havre. In my mind I could almost reconstruct what had happened to Gillis and Jackson. Not realizing their terrific southward drift, they must have reached the Channel in the vicinity of the islands off Cherbourg, and assuming them to be the Frisian Islands 600 miles to the north, would have turned south into the Bay of Biscay toward Spain. As incredible as it sounds this is exactly what happened. I reached 30,000 feet over Normandy, and drifted southwest toward the Brest Peninsula as I listened intently on "A" channel, our squadron frequency. As I approached the tip of the peninsula my heart bounded as I faintly heard a drawling voice say disgustedly, "Where in the *hell* are we, Jackson?"

"I don't know, Gillis. I've got my escape kit map out, but I can't find anything like that on it. I think we're lost!"

At this time they were at 30,000 feet, and were looking in puzzlement at the northern Spanish coast coming into view to the south of them. I raised them immediately, calling them by name and flight designation. "Hallum, Green 3 and 4, Jackson and Gillis, this is Hallum Red 1, calling! Do you read me?"

Then I heard Gillis: "Hey, Jackson! I think I heard Major Turner call just then!"

"Yeah! I heard him too! Hello, Red 1 this is Green 3 and 4. We're lost! Where are you?"

I was so happy that I almost laughed as I replied, "I'm north of you at the tip of the Brest Peninsula. How's your gas? Do you have enough to return to England? You are halfway down to Spain. Turn 180 degrees and come north. I'll pick you up and lead you home!"

I heard them discussing their gas supply, and the feasibility of landing in Spain; then the slow Texas drawl of Gillis broke up the discussion. "Aw, hell, let's go home. I'm tired 'n hungry."

Taking this as a decision I instructed them to come north in a slow descent, and to set their prop controls to 1700 rpm with as much manifold pressure as the engine would take. This combination would extend their range to the utmost. By now they had been in the air continuously for seven hours, and I knew it would be close. Now I looked at my map, and picked out the airfield at Gosport, just north of the Isle of Wight, as the nearest that I could lead them to. About this time near disaster struck.

In getting my Mustang refueled, I had forgotten to order the oxygen supply replenished. Now it ran out without warning, and I blacked out at 30,000 feet. I must have spun for at least 20,000 feet, for my next clear thought came as I watched what I thought was a funny-looking green sky swirling round and round. "That's no sky! That's the *ocean!*" Then calls from Gillis and Jackson over the RT jerked me back to reality. The denser air at 10,000 feet revived me, enabling me to recover automatically from the spin. If there were any observers watching from the peninsula they must have been mightily puzzled by the antics of a nutty American Mustang alone in enemy airspace.

I reassured Gillis and Jackson that I was watching for them, and squared myself away at about 6000 feet. I was heading for a spot in the southern English Channel about fifty miles south of the Isle of Wight where I hoped to intercept my boys. Approaching the spot I found a peculiar-looking object suspended in the sky at twelve o'clock low. Nearing it, I saw that it was a barrage balloon which had evidently slipped its mooring and had drifted out to sea. It couldn't have been better if I had planned it, and I called to Jackson and Gillis telling them of the balloon. I had no sooner ended my transmission when I heard Jackson exclaim, "I see it. There it is dead ahead of us twelve o'clock level."

I cut in and told them I would pick them up as they passed the barrage balloon, and started a turn toward them as I saw another sight which chilled my rising spirits. Off to my right I saw a lone fighter boring toward the direction of my strays. I flushed with anger, thinking it was a ME-109. "I'll be damned if I'm going to lose them now after all this!" I pulled around in a tight turn flipping on my gun switch and sight as I took a slight quartering lead on the approaching fighter. Evidently he hadn't seen me for he was fast approaching the "cold meat" position. I couldn't miss, and would blow him to hell with the first burst. Just as I was about to squeeze the trigger something about the aircraft's shape made me hesitate, and in that split-second I recognized it for a Spitfire—one of ours! Frantically I nosed down under it and in a screaming climbing turn settled alongside of him, rocking my wings frantically to get his attention. He now saw me for the first time at this point, for he almost did a snap roll in his startled reaction as he saw me. Jackson and Gillis had now passed the balloon headed for the Isle of Wight and the Spitfire and I circled them. The Spitfire must have been sent out by the English Coastal Command to intercept the three strange blips we created on their radar. I flew above and to the front of Gillis and Jackson giving them corrections in course so that they would waste no gas on the way to Gosport. By now they had been aloft for eight hours and must be flying on fumes.

Sighting Gosport I had Gillis and Jackson get in line astern for a straight-in landing, and I switched to the common VHF radio channel for all airfields, requesting Gosport tower to give them emergency clearance. Gillis landed first and taxied to a parking ramp. Jackson lost power on the final stages of his approach, but completed his landing although he nosed up and bent his prop at the last minute.

They were both safely down, and the Spitfire and I now landed ourselves. Jackson and Gillis had been in the air for eight and a half continuous hours—an almost unbelievable time range, even for a Mustang. Upon returning to base with my two pilots we found that the three others, Lieutenant Edward Regis, Lieutenant Franklyn Hendrickson, and Lieutenant Joseph Lilly, were still missing, and were presumed to be down in enemy territory. I was sorry to learn this, but was supremely pleased and happy to have my own two boys back home safe and sound. To me it was a very satisfactory mission. Again

I received a half-hearted reprimand from Group at having charged off without formal permission, but under the circumstances I would have been happy in view of the results to take a bust in rank. Later the reprimand was reversed, and instead they awarded me a cluster to my Distinguished Flying Cross for my action in the affair.

Next day the group flew two dive-bombing missions in France, one to Charleroi and one to Creil. I flew the one to Creil; but neither of the missions produced enemy air action. The pilots, however, appreciated having a short run to fly for a change.

I didn't fly the last mission of the month, on the 30th. It was a penetration sweep to Lyon, France, with no claims and no losses. As the fifth month of combat for the Group vanished into history our Group record stood at 250 German aircraft destroyed, sixty-two pilots killed or missing in action and sixty-six combat missions flown.

The month of May was a busy month, but a lean one for me. The Group destroyed seventy-five more German planes, but most of them were bagged in five or six missions, which made the remainder tail weary experiences, for the most part, with little enemy action to liven them up. This, of course, was ideal for bombers, but for us fighters it meant hour upon hour of routine patrol, unable to move in the cramped cockpit. I seldom even got a glimpse of the enemy. It seems I either missed the missions where a fight developed or I was on the wrong side of the bomber stream to be part of a big engagement.

Our work was divided about equally during the month between long-range heavy escort, short-range medium (B-26) escort and dive-bombing with a little strafing thrown in to keep from dying of boredom. The one mission of the month, May 28, 1944, that produced the best action was one which I naturally missed out on the action. I missed the heavy fighting, but had an unusual and interesting contact with the enemy. We were on heavy escort duty south of Magdeburg, Germany. I led the 356th which was to protect against attacks from the south of the bomber stream. I had deployed White flight to the side and just below bomber level, Blue flight ahead of bomber stream, Green flight to the rear, and I held my own Red flight above at 30,000 feet midway along the bomber stream to enable me to dive to any of these areas if necessary as source of main attack or thrust by enemy aircraft.

After sweeping our deployed areas for a while we began to hear RT reports from the 355th and 353rd Squadrons of contacts with the enemy to the north, and soon it was clear that flights in the north sector beyond the bomber stream were heavily engaged in a knock-down-drag-out fight with ME-109s and Focke-Wulf-190s. By now we were eager and ready, anticipating similar action in our own southern sector of defense. But time slipped by and it failed to develop. From experience we knew a battle of the evident magnitude we heard to the north would normally extend throughout the entire area. For some inexplicable reason, nevertheless, the fighting seemed to be drifting to the north, away from us. The bombers were delighted no doubt, but my boys and I were in a frenzy, darting from place to place within our sector hoping to cut in on a piece of the action dangling so near and yet out of reach. There is no torture comparable to that suffered by a fighter pilot forced to *listen* to a nearby aerial action which he cannot join. We couldn't abandon our sector; so we sat uncomfortably for thirty minutes. I had just about reconciled to "no contact" and was thinking about taking the squadron home when my wingman, Red 2, reported a bogie at three o'clock. Turning to the reported sighting, I found the bogie, a tiny speck now at twelve o'clock level. In a surprisingly short time it resolved itself as a twin-engine aircraft paralleling the bomber stream. Now it looked like a pregnant ME-109, but no one could identify it positively at our range.

We were doing about 410 mph true airspeed but now with mild surprise I noted that the bogie was steadily pulling ahead of us. I asked Blue flight to swing west and watch for the bogie coming fast at 30,000 feet. I then alerted White and Green flights to watch for very fast twin-engined aircraft, advising them to stay between it and the bombers to force a head-on attack. I had a feeling we couldn't catch this rascal in a chase, and if he got by us he would have a field day with the lumbering bombers. Every pilot became aware of the unusual aspect of the bogie when I ordered head-on tactics. It had remained our policy as a group never to break off a head-on attack. Most of us were witnesses when our original commander, Colonel Martin went down over Frankfurt demonstrating what he preached. By now the bogie had discovered our Blue flight coming west edging out to hit him with a head-on pass. The bogie turned to his right 180 degrees away from the bombers traveling west now. During his turn I had cut the corner on him making him drift even farther south. Green flight had come east from the rear of the bomber stream until they had sighted us and located the bogie at two o'clock.

Now we had the German trapped in a huge triangle with forty-eight 50-caliber machine guns at its corners. I told all flight leaders if the bogie tried to dive under us for the bombers each leader with his wingman would intercept him, leaving element leaders and their wingmen to cut him off as he turned away from us. But the bogie had good eyes, and must have seen Green flight coming up from the west. The odds of 12 to 1 did not appeal to him. He pulled up in a chandelle to the south and entered a 60-degree dive down and away from us. With his amazing speed he disappeared before we could pursue, so I called the flights back to the bomber stream which had now completed its bombing run, and was heading back toward the Channel area. Contact with the bogie had consumed about twenty minutes, and the strange thing was that at no time were we able tc close near enough to get a positive identification of the aircraft. I knew from forty-nine missions worth of experience that Jerry had some damned good pilots, so I chalked this cagey devil up as one of their old hands, probably in a souped up JU-88, who had acquired more brains than patriotism. Later upon reflection I decided that this elusive bogie of the Magdeburg mission could have been the German jet, the ME-262 which we had heard about through intelligence reports, but which we had not seen previously in the air. In retrospect I cannot remember a fight as big as that which took place to the north of the bomber stream that day failing to filter through the entire area eventually after the swirl of combat had its dispersion effect. Now, my conclusion is that German fighters were ordered to draw all Allied fighters to the north, leaving the south approach free for the single swift

ME-262 which could have dealt havoc among the bombers. If that *was* an ME-262 I'm eternally grateful that there was only one of them up there that day; for with even two of them, had they coordinated their attack, it would have been nearly impossible for us to fend them off. Even later when the ME-262s were to be expected it was common knowledge that the only tactical defense against them was to stay between them and the bombers—if possible—and use our shorter radius-of-turn to block their thrusts and force them to run a gauntlet of head-on attack to get to the bombers. The only other alternatives were to catch them on the ground, taking off, landing or coasting for base out of fuel.

Upon return to Maidstone we learned that the others in the group had indeed fought a big one with the enemy, twenty enemy aircraft were claimed. Alone Captain Wally Emmer of the 353rd accounted for three and one-half. We had lost two planes and their pilots, Lieutenant Glenn Pipes and Lieutenant Don McDowell from the 353rd.

CHAPTER 7

Since the 25th of May the group had been informed officially that it was now on a six-hour alert status, and had been assigned two officers from General Patton's Third Army to stay with us and set up ground liaison procedures. There were a rash of secret staff meetings and assignments of enlisted men to special transportation waterproofing schools all of which pointed plainly that something special was in the breeze. Our flying hadn't changed much except that more dive-bombing, fighter sweeps and strafing missions were being thrown in with our normal escort duties, and this stepped up the pace of operations somewhat.

It didn't take much brainpower to guess that the invasion of the Continent was imminent. The clincher came when we discovered a small detail of cameramen among us who had been assigned to cover our first day activities on "D-Day." On the 3rd and 4th of June a couple of short missions were run over France. Rumor and speculation ran high on the 5th and 6th of June as we awaited the event with bated breath, and when it was revealed that the first days operations on the invasion had already been completed without our participation we felt very much let down.

Our fighting spirit came to peak pitch again, when after supper on the 6th we were summarily summoned to an immediate briefing. We found that we were to escort a C-47 and glider mission that night. We were to man our planes immediately, and to remain in them ready to take off upon signal from the tower. We were in our Mustangs at nine o'clock that evening and at ten we finally got the green "take-off" flare.

Forming up in the settling dusk proved to be no problem, and when we rendezvoused with the southbound C-47s and gliders a half hour later over southern England we could still see them fairly well in the twilight. My flight had a "box" of sixteen C-47s and gliders to escort, and by the time we passed over the coastline and the Isle of Wight it was black as the ace of spades. A cloud cover obscured even the faint starlight. The only way I could keep track of my charges was to concentrate on the blue flame of their engine exhausts. This was a pretty tense way to provide escort, and I couldn't help wondering just how I was supposed to tell the difference between our planes and theirs if the Germans attempted an interception. I left that problem to be solved when it arrived, and strained to stay with my C-47s and gliders without running them down in the process.

When we got to mid-Channel we were supposed to turn east, and proceed off Cherbourg where the C-47s and gliders were to penetrate the enemy coast. Normally escorting fighters move in advance of convoyed planes also, but tonight we were strictly followers, glued close to our charges hoping they knew where we were. I divided my time between keeping one eye fixed on the ghostly C-47s, avoiding the deadly tow line between them and the gliders, and apprehensively watching for other wandering escorting fighters that frequently cut in front of us. Altogether it was a cliff hanging mess! Luckily, I caught the turn made by the C-47s eastward up the middle of the Channel, and was able to stay with them. After two and a half hours of this kind of heart-seizing flying we finally crossed in over the coastline, and the C-47s cut loose their gliders and dropped their paratroopers. I knew the mission had been completed only because without warning the air burst into a maelstrom of crisscrossing tracer fire from the void below. I made a sweeping level turn to the right with my flight away from the drop zone, and beat it for the southern coast of England.

Yet now we were presented with an even stickier problem. I knew our group alone had forty-eight churning Mustangs in the black void ahead, and all of them were converging for the pundit light at Christchurch for landing and refueling there before returning to home base. The pundit light was a powerful hooded searchlight throwing its beam straight up into the sky, a marker for friendly aircraft. The beam is invisible until you are directly over it, and there would be terrifically heavy congestion over it tonight. We were briefed to orbit the light, and take our turn to land at nearby Christchurch, but with the milling horde of fighters I knew this procedure was SNAFU. God alone knows how many planes from other Groups were being diverted to the same rendezvous light, and it was with mounting apprehension that I approached the Bournemouth area to search the blackness for the pundit. There had already been six hair-raising near-collisions with other homeward-bound flights. As we flew on I debated chucking the whole mess to fly directly to our own base, but I finally resolved to follow the mission flight plan, even if it killed us all—as it well could!

It was a case of which was greater, your patience or your fear; and I must admit my patience was wearing exceedingly thin. After discovering the light by merest chance, I flew a wide and careful orbit around the area avoiding other fighters that loomed near us. Finding the runway at Christchurch I decided that the safest way to land my flight intact was to use a 1000-foot overhead 360-degree landing pattern in formation. This was not the usual system used, but it would keep the flight together, which on such a night was essential for our safety. With the flight kept in close formation while landing it would be easier for individual fighters to see us, and make them more inclined to give way by force of numbers. The system worked perfectly. I set up the flight in close formation 1000 feet over the runway with wheels and flaps down, and flew a wide descending circle with carefully slow power reductions finally skimming the approach end of the runway in perfect formation. We had it made! Cutting power at my voice signal the flight settled in for touchdown, and rolled to the intersection where we turned as one and taxied individually to the parking ramp. As you can see the pilots in my squadron were of the best. They could and did perform any maneuver I ever asked of them.

I strolled into the Base Operations Office and there found Colonel Bickell who had already come in. He beckoned to me to join them, and I learned that because of the difficulty in landing fighters that night the Ninth Air Force was worried about having the available men and planes for a scheduled patrol of the beachhead at dawn. The upshot was that they asked me to collect the members of my squadron who had landed tonight, and to take off at dawn to provide fighter cover of the beach for a two-hour period. That would give them time to get things squared away and back on regular scheduling. This was a chance to see the Invasion at firsthand, and I jumped at it.

I found three of my flights on the ground. Hastily I arranged for refueling of our Mustangs, and scrounged bunks in a nearby barracks so we could sack out for three or four hours at least. Shortly before dawn I assembled my pilots in the operations office and briefed them. The plan was now to fly straight to the beachhead to provide air coverage from the mouth of the Seine to the Cherbourg Peninsula for one hour. Taking off we found the cloud cover had dropped somewhat and we were forced to fly at about 4000 feet. Crossing the Channel I saw the debris of what looked to me to be C-47s floating forlornly on the oily water, a grim reminder of last night's mission. Arriving over the bay of the Seine we could see ships, boats and LSTs spread out for miles, extending out of sight into the Channel. As we started over them toward the beach I took care to give all large ships a wide berth, rocking my wings vigorously to show we were friendly. At this low altitude they could clobber us if they mistakenly fired upon us. As far as I was concerned they were just big floating flak factories. None of the warships fired but we did draw a few shots from trigger-happy gunners on smaller craft before someone aboard silenced them.

As we drifted back and forth patrolling the beach I could see a helter-skelter collection of matériel and vehicles scattered on the beaches in varying concentrations, and I could see a steady movement of personnel through the beaches to the inland woods. All looked orderly and peaceful from 4000 feet where we were flying, but now and then a half-sunken ship, a burning vehicle or some unidentifiable wreckage would be visible. I noticed the wreckage of a C-47 and a P-47 which had been forced to use the beach as a landing surface. After our first sweep of the area we started looking for the German fighters we expected to find trying to hit the invasion forces, but except for ourselves the sky was empty. The only German aircraft I saw tried to sneak in at water level from the northeast in the direction of Dieppe only to be caught in murderous cross fire from two big cruisers, and it fell into the Channel in a long splash of flame. I led the flight up toward the crash site in hopes of finding other venturesome Nazis. We saw no more fighters, however, until a squadron of P-47s arrived to relieve us. I gathered my Mustangs, and flew up the French coast to Calais where we jumped across the Strait of Dover to our base at Maidstone. We arrived in time for lunch, and to find that our squadron was scheduled for another C-47 and glider escort mission that afternoon.

Later, after briefing, we flew down to the southern tip of England again and picked up another long string of "Gooney Birds" dragging gliders, and took them across the Channel to Utah Beach where they penetrated five or ten miles and cut their gliders loose. I watched the gliders in fascination as they made their tight little spirals to the terrain below. They didn't really waste much time gliding, and many of the landings I saw looked pretty rough. Knowing that the glider pilots had to join the ground troops to fight their way out, it seemed to be a pretty rugged job they were doing, and as we took the C-47s back out to the Channel I thanked the Lord again for making me a simple fighter pilot.

I didn't fly again until the 10th of June when we escorted another paratroop drop behind Utah Beach. It was an uneventful mission for us since the German aircraft were still nowhere to be seen. On our return flight we utilized the range of our Mustangs to roam deep behind the beachhead to shoot at railroads, roads, supply dumps or whatever we could find that would hinder the German defenses. Nothing was safe on the road that day for we strafed anything that moved. We landed at Maidstone five hours later feeling like we had begun to earn our pay again, for at last we had used our guns.

On the 12th of June all three squadrons were given dive-bombing targets in northern France. The target of the 356th was a railway bridge near Rouen. I took off with the squadron anticipating another cut-and-dried mission. Flying straight to the target area I found the bridge, and orbited it at 5000 feet checking for flak emplacements to determine whether a concentrated or a coordinated attack should be used. A "concentrated" attack with the squadron using the same diving line was preferred for effectiveness and accuracy since each pilot could guide his drop by the drop ahead of his own. A short or a long drop would still tear up track line even if it missed the primary target of the bridge. On the other hand, if a target was obviously well-defended by flak positions you could minimize your own losses by organizing a "coordinated" attack. In a coordinated attack the forces were divided and approached the target at close intervals from different directions, thus confusing the defensive forces. If the flak defense appeared to be particularly heavy sometimes a single flight strafing the flak positions just a second prior to the dive-bombing would do wonders in rendering the flak ineffective. A little on the spot target reconnaissance paid big dividends in keeping your pilots in one piece. Those were the kind I wanted; besides, my squadron-mates were all good friends.

Today I could find no traces of flak positions, and we set up a concentrated attack and plastered the bridge, but good! After the attack I flew back over it alone to check results after the smoke and debris had cleared. We had hit it with thirty-two 500-pounders, and most of them must have scored well, for at both ends the tracks ended with twisted stubs with the intervening bridge crumpled into the canyon below. Turning northeast I decided to take the squadron around the countryside for a little predatory hunting.

There had been reports received of enemy aircraft in this general area of France, and I felt that a look-see couldn't hurt. Within fifteen minutes I heard someone in the squadron exclaim excitedly over the RT, "There's a great big pasture down there at three o'clock with a whole flock of FW-190s tailed into the hedgerows!"

Stabbing my eyes downward to the right, sure enough, there was a large field, and parked fighters poked their tails in scattered groups out of the foliage of the hedgerows. Quickly checking the area I couldn't see any flak positions so I called to the squadron to follow me, and rolled over into a dive. As the nearest line of five FW-190s crept into range I fired off long bursts and slowly let my fire "walk" through them as I bore down upon them. Before long two had caught fire and were obscuring the others billowing smoke. I pulled upward from the deck in a shallow turning climb to the left, and saw ahead of me, alongside another hedgerow, a single FW-190 being refueled from a truck. Rolling out level and depressing the nose of the Mustang I let fly with another hard burst of .50s. Within seconds the truck exploded in a brilliant flash, engulfing the hapless aircraft. Pulling up again I observed that my team had established an orbital traffic pattern around the perimeter of the field. They looked like a circle of Yo-yos as they bobbed up and down taking shots at targets of opportunity. At my low altitude I could see a number of undamaged targets; so I joined the pattern of the flight to help torch them. After four more firing passes I began to get an uneasy feeling about the time we were spending at this one spot; for our very target proved that there were German fighters in the area, and we could be caught like a bunch of fat sitting ducks. I zoomed upward to look around the horizon. As I passed 1500 feet I saw a dust trail in another field ten hedgerows away. Calling to my squadron to break off their strafing for assembly at 10,000 feet, I headed in a shallow dive for the dust cloud ahead. I discovered the dust came from a JU-88 on its take-off run. He probably saw me coming, because he set his plane back on the ground. I hit him just as he rolled to a stop, and he exploded.

With our ammo practically expended and signs of a

hornet's nest being stirred up by our activities, it was time for "Ole Dick" and his boys to hit the trail for home. Safe back at base with no damage or losses we sorted out the results. Besides the bridge, the squadron reported a count of twenty burning FW-190s, and with my bonus JU-88, the total destroyed ran to twenty-one. It was a satisfactory day's work.

On the 13th we were informed that we would soon be moved cross Channel to an advanced fighter strip on the beachhead, in order to give close support to the Army advance. Thus our work with the Eighth Air Force came to its conclusion. We continued our operations under the 19th Tactical Air Command of Brigadier General Otto P. Weyland.

At 11:45 P.M. on the 15th most of the group was rudely awakened to the terror of Germany's first "Secret Weapon," the V-1, or Flying Bomb. We were sleeping peacefully in our bivouac areas when we were literally bounced from our sacks by the muzzle blasts and thunderous reverberations of nearby 90-mm gun emplacements. We had seen these emplacements around the area, but had never heard them fire before. It was a bizarre half hour before we found the reason for the excitement. The gunners were shooting at V-1s buzzing overhead toward London. The V-1s had pre-set gyroscopic guidance systems which kept them on an unwavering course to London, and the fuel was calculated to run out in a pre-set area. The pulsating putter of the V-1s ram jet engine sounded like a very loud motorcycle going wide out. As long as you could hear them you were safe, but when the engine sound cut off abruptly, they were going into their final destructive dive. Their blast effect was tremendous. These missiles kept us on edge every night until we left for our beachhead, Strip A-2 near Grand-Camp-les-Bains on the Normandy coast.

In the early morning of the 18th of June we ran a dive-bombing mission into France which was completed within two hours. On the return trip to base I hovered my flight in a loose orbit at 6000 feet between Calais and Dover. With plenty of fuel and ammunition left, I was tempted to subtract a few buzz bombs from the many the Germans were sending over to terrorize London. They traveled at an altitude of between 2000 and 3000 feet, and cruised at speeds of 300 to 500 mph. I felt if we could pick them up over the Channel and dive on them, we stood a good chance of knocking them down since they were unable to evade us in any way. I sighted one below and dived on it, pulling out behind it but slightly out of range. I tried to close the distance, but the missile was just a little too fast. I chased the infernal machine for ten minutes alternately diving to gain speed, and pulling up to lob long-range bursts at it. Eventually one of my bullets must have scored a chance hit in the engine, for suddenly it emitted a long streamer of yellow flame and lost speed quickly. In a curving dive, it plunged into a vacant field below where it exploded harmlessly. Encouraged by my success I proceeded back to the Channel area to pick up another. I began to wonder how I was going to get the next V-1, because most of my ammo was expended, and my gun barrels had burnt out. Soon I saw another one and made a very steep dive to gain extra overtaking speed. This bomb must have been moving more slowly than the first one, for I almost overran it as I pulled out of my dive. As I flew alongside of the little monster I had a new idea. I knew they were controlled by a gyro guidance "brain," and perhaps this mechanism could be upset without gunfire. I carefully edged close to it and placed my wingtip about a foot under its tiny fin. Rolling my plane suddenly neatly flipped the V-1 upside-down, and it promptly spun into the shallows of the Channel near the English shore where it blew a useless hole in the water. Jubilant with my success I flew back to Maidstone and hastened to tell the other pilots of the new pastime I had discovered.

CHAPTER 8

On June 19 the group flew all of its aircraft to its new base, Strip A-2 on the beachhead in Normandy. An advanced detachment from each squadron had previously been sent to the strip to prepare it for our occupation. This apparently routine movement of our operational aircraft from Maidstone to Strip A-2 provided me with fifteen seconds of the most hair-raising flying experience I was to have in the ETO.

Reports had been received from our advanced echelon party about their difficulty in locating a source of pure water. I therefore decided that the 356th fighters flown to the strip would carry drop tanks filled not with gas but with good water in an effort to alleviate an acute shortage. With my twenty-five fighters we could bring with us over 3600 extra gallons of potable water for the immediate use of the squadron. This plan was carried out by our puzzled crew chiefs who attached the tanks and filled them with water, and I led my squadron on the short journey to Strip A-2.

Just prior to take-off the Group finance officer rushed up to me and asked if I would carry a large paper sack over with me in my cockpit to Strip A-2, to be given to my squadron adjutant. I told him that I would be glad to, and incidentally asked what the sack contained. I was startled to learn that it held $75,000 in cash to be used for the payroll formation scheduled shortly. The squadron had an aggregate armament of one hundred 50-caliber machine guns to protect this shipment of bullion, and I couldn't help thinking of old frontier stagecoaches transporting similar cargo protected only by a scared cowboy with a shotgun.

Arriving over Strip A-2 we found one north-south runway carved into the hedgerows covered with interlocking metal-pierced planking. Checking the windsock I found we would be landing to the north. I put the six squadron flights in line astern and made a pass over the runway for peel off. There was a camouflaged tower truck about mid-strip on the west side of the runway, and I learned over the RT that there would be a traffic control jeep parked near the runway on the approach to give red flares to any congestion that might develop. After peel off I set up my Mustang in routine manner on the downwind circuit with wheels and flaps down, preparing for touchdown normally at the south end of the runway. I had no suspicion of trouble as I straightened out at about 40 feet altitude, 100 feet short of the runway. Just then my mistake caught up with me. In most previous landings I had been returning from missions with my fuel almost expended, giving me a lightened condition, and I had unconsciously set up my gliding speed for such a landing. Now, however, I had almost a full load of fuel, plus two drop tanks loaded with water—even heavier than fuel—and the normal gliding speed just wasn't enough to keep me flying. The plane reacted with a sudden lurch of the left wing, and stalled 50 feet from the runway, 25 feet in the air. My instinctive reaction was to shove the throttle forward to the wall, gingerly playing the stick and rudder controls against the stall pressures, in a desperate endeavor to keep the shuddering craft airborne. The plane nosed high and, wallowing drunkenly from side to side, strayed to the left toward the runway jeep control, where two pilots hastily sought safer ground. The engine power finally reasserted itself, but I seemed to have trouble pulling up the left wing. It took full right rudder and right aileron to force the plane up to the horizontal position where at about 50 feet altitude I roared down the runway regaining airspeed. By the time I reached the end of the runway I had regained control of the ship as well as my blood pressure. Sheepishly, I called the squadron to remind them that landing speed would be about 15 mph higher on account of the water load. O'Connor asked whether the acrobatics on the final approach were required, to which I replied in the negative. Tommy, my crew chief, stood at the left wingtip regarding it with a puzzled air! Looking too, I found I had scraped the navigation light off, leaving a long groove six to eight inches deep gouged in the tip. Out at the runway control jeep, the two pilots showed me a foot-deep trench in the loose earth, stretching 20 yards in the approach clearing where I had dragged the wingtip before regaining control. No wonder it had been difficult to pull up the left wing! It was a narrow escape, and if I had applied power a fraction of a second later, I probably wouldn't have been able to recover. Ironically, it turned out that there was plenty of good fresh water available, and my improvised aerial waterpipe had been a case of "carrying coal to Newcastle."

For the next four days I was occupied getting the squadron settled. We established our squadron area, consisting of bivouac, engineering, transportation, supply, mess, operations, and headquarters. Bivouac consisted of designating locations for men and officers where deep foxholes were dug for sleeping.

The front line was only ten miles to the south, and we were told that there was a definite possibility of sniper fire in the area, especially after twilight hours. During the night we could hear the rumble of combat and see occasional flashes of light in the south. In England, outside of a few night air raids, none of the group but the pilots had ever experienced eerie and unsettling fear which accompanies nearby combat action. There was no outward expression of this fear, but each man was aware that enemy forces were within striking distance, and that the immediate future was in the hands of fate. This knowledge kept everyone on his toes. Top efficiency and cooperation were maintained with little urging. It amazed me to witness the teamwork of all these men in a smoothly operating unit under the adversity and pressure of combat conditions. A determination to accomplish the mission at hand with selfless effort was the rule rather than the exception. The bounds of human endeavor are limitless when the cause is meaningful.

In a comparatively short time and with a lot of hard work, the squadron area began to shape up, and eventually we moved from the foxholes to a flimsy but comfortable tent.

Once again the ingenuity of my men proved itself,

when as if by magic they produced showerheads and all the necessary plumbing to construct shower stalls complete with hot and cold running water. I wasn't surprised to learn that my squadron had the first shower facilities on the beachhead, though it didn't take the other two squadrons long to copy the idea. We even had a cleaning and pressing service operated (with my tacit permission) by Corporal Robert D. Berge—a crafty midnight entrepreneur—who always seemed to have something going for himself. Knowing Berge, I didn't dare investigate his operations too closely for fear that I might have to court martial him if I knew his source of supplies. I was sure Corporal Berge would make a million after the war—that is if he wasn't shot by some irate property owner in the meantime. Having constructed the squadron Enlisted Men's Club and the Officers' Club, we had all the conveniences of any military base, though ours were slightly less permanent than most.

Our combat missions consisted mainly of fighter sweeps, beach patrols, dive-bombing, close support for ground elements, armed reconnaissance, and an occasional B-26 escort. Most of these missions were carried out by separate squadrons flying to different targets, and we had very few of the old group missions which we had become accustomed to on heavy bomber escort duty. The new set-up served to unify individual squadrons, as they ran missions as fighting units independent of other squadron action. But we all missed the big aerial battles with the Germans that the old group missions yielded. Contact with the enemy in the air was now scarce. When we did run into the Germans, it was usually in surprise meetings with one or two wanderers, since there was no bomber stream to coax them up to us in numbers. In a word, the hunting was lousy, and we had to make the most of limited opportunities.

On June 24 and 25 I led the 356th on fighter sweeps to the Margny-Le Haye De Puits areas north of Paris, but our luck was sour, and we returned to A-2 without contacting the enemy.

The only German aircraft we had seen since beginning operations on the beachhead was bedcheck "Charlie," a particularly irritating 109 who had the habit of flying across the lines around ten or eleven o'clock at night after most of us had sacked out. His arrival over the field invariably aroused the fire of every trigger happy ack-ack gunner for miles around. The resulting din would have made a night in a boiler factory sound like a whispering wind. The worst part of it was watching his progress—which was marked by the probing tracers and bursting flak—without a chance of getting a crack at him ourselves.

Antiaircraft batteries were not the most popular organizations among those of us who were pilots. The natural aversion we held for those engaged in our personal destruction was heightened somewhat by this incident which we witnessed one evening on our own airstrip. It was understood by all pilots that we must return to base at least one hour before dark from any mission, and it was the responsibility of the mission leader to see that this rule was carried out. The reason for this rule was twofold: first, our advanced strip had no night lighting, and second, the gun crews of the antiaircraft batteries surrounding our area found it difficult to distinguish between our own planes and those of the enemy in the failing light of twilight. This particular day, shortly after

21. "Pioneer Mustang" aces. From Frantz (with mustache) to the right: Brueland, O'Connor, Goodnight, Emmer, Beerbower, Bradley, Eagleston, Stephens, myself, and Hunt. Aggregate confirmed kills in the huddle: 108.

26. Author escorting "Big Friends" B-17s deep over Germany.

27. General O. P. Weyland presents a cluster to the 354th Fighter Group's Presidential Unit Citation.

24. and 25. Saint-Lo, France, before and after the Allied breakthrough.

22. Jim Howard's P-51B "Ding Hao," named in honor of his "Number One" experience with the Flying Tigers in China and Burma in 1941–42.

23. "Stars Look Down" was an appropriate name for the P-51B with jump seat behind the pilot which was used to fly General Eisenhower on a personal reconnaissance over Saint-Lo before the breakthrough.

our arrival in France, all Group aircraft had returned and landed well before dark, having completed our combat activity for the day.

After mess, I was on the flight line checking with engineering on my fighter status for the next morning's mission. Dusk was falling as I heard the whistling of a P-38s engines approaching the strip. Surprised that one of our own fighters was so low over the beachhead this late in the day, I rushed outside the engineering office to check what was happening. There were no P-38s based in the beachhead area as yet, and as far as I knew we were the only fighter group based here, so I assumed this to be an Eighth Air Force fighter returning from a heavy escort mission who had gotten lost, or was running low on gas and was looking for shelter at our landing strip. As I looked up, I saw the unmistakable silhouette of a single P-38 circling the airstrip. Praying for the pilot to speed up his landing, I took off at a run for the mobile truck tower, shouting for them to give the 38 a green light for landing. Then I remembered with concern the multitude of light and heavy ack-ack sites surrounding the field, and yelled back to someone in the engineering tent to alert the AAA Command that the fighter overhead was an American, and was not to be fired on.

Holding my breath, I watched the 38 as he continued to make careful circuits of the strip as if he were wondering whether or not he had been recognized as one of our own. Evidently, he had either made contact with the tower or had received the green light from them, for he settled into a slow downwind leg, and dropped his landing gear. I grinned broadly, knowing the relief the lonely pilot must be feeling at having made it in. I continued to watch the plane as it turned onto its base leg, and then onto the final approach. About 500 feet from the end of the runway the pilot flipped on his landing lights, which was routine procedure. This time, unfortunately, the routine was to result in tragedy. Evidently, some unalert gunner in the perimeter defenses had been unaware that an aircraft was even in the landing pattern, and as the landing lights flashed on suddenly in the enveloping darkness, he was startled into firing. His tracers arched toward the 38, but fell far short of their mark. Had this been the only gun to fire, the 38 might have still made a safe landing, but the first shots caused every other gunner to open fire on the hapless fighter.

Stunned by the horrifying spectacle, and sick at my inability to prevent it, I ran stumbling and yelling toward the nearest source of tracer fire, trying to stop their fire. My attempts were in vain. The poor pilot had reacted instantly to the crisscross of fire which enveloped his plane, and flipped off his landing lights, trying desperately to raise his gear and maneuver the plane, straining the engine for more flying speed to escape the storm of fire. He made a heroic effort, managing to fly the length of the runway unhit, and was about to slip into the shelter of the dark night, when a flash of fire flared around his right engine, causing the plane to shudder and crash to earth.

Like a contrite watchdog caught barking at an old family friend, the antiaircraft fire barked and stuttered to a whimpering silence but too late. The damage had been done. In spite of all of man's careful plans to establish safeguards against human error, war sometimes creates situations that make a tragic mockery of such plans. It is not so surprising, then, that those intimately engaged in combat so often adopt a fatalistic attitude to protect themselves from these shocks to the mind. I stood in the middle of the runway watching the point where the P-38 had disappeared for a long while, overcome with bitterness and despondency at my fruitless efforts to aid the stricken man. I knew in my heart that it was all a horribly tragic mistake, but this couldn't assuage the immense frustration I felt. Finally, I slowly returned to my squadron area with heavy heart.

On June 28, I led two flights of my squadron on an assault-area patrol of the beachhead. The weather was fair, with scattered cloud cover at about 10,000 feet, which required that we set our patrol altitude beneath the cloud cover at 8000, to keep sight of beach activity and be ready to counter any German air attacks which might develop. This situation denied us the opportunity to fly at high altitudes where from past experience we could expect to find the enemy. I wasn't too optimistic about combat engagement. But there was always a good chance of random surprise meetings, and this kept us alert and constantly searching for any telltale signs which might lead us to a good fight. For about an hour we flew a very uneventful patrol. I was offshore near Bayeux, flying east toward Le Havre when I caught sight of six aircraft diving from the base of the cloud cover over Le Havre. I called the bogies in to the patrol flights, and increased to combat power as I flipped the gun switch and sight on.

As the speed increased, I made an "S" turn to the left, in order to approach the bogies in a quartering head-on attack from the left which would give me a better chance to identify them. I could see now that they were heading in our direction, and that one was far out ahead of the others. In a few seconds I identified the lead plane as a 109, and recognized the others to be English Spitfires. Excitement raced through me now as I gauged the distance between the Spits and the 109. If he turned back to Le Havre, which was out of my patrol area, I'd have to let the Spits have him. But if he came on to the Caen area he'd be entering my territory, and the Spits would have to take pot luck. Any German fighter in my patrol area was fair game, and I wasn't planning to waste time being polite to our allies. As it turned out, I was downright rude. The 109 pilot saw us coming, and turned south toward Caen. Forgetting the Spitfires and everything else but my prey, I whipped over in a steep right turn and latched onto the tail of the 109 sandwiching myself between him and the Spits. Naturally, my flights followed, and the Spitfires had to pull up and abandon the chase or get run over by a herd of Mustangs. I had my engine wide open now, and was overtaking the 109. As I came into range, I settled the sight pip on the top of his rudder, and fired a short experimental burst from my 50s. I must have been skidding slightly, for I only nicked him in the wingtip which caused him to pull up in a shallow climbing turn to the left, toward the cloud base over Caen. My range was closing fast now, and I followed him in his turn, and led him a little before I squeezed the trigger again. This time, just as he reached the base of the clouds, I scored a thick cluster of strike hits which ranged from his wing root to the engine nacelle, and he left a trail of fire and smoke as he zoomed into the opaque darkness of the cloud base.

Half a second later the tumbling body of the pilot dropped from the clouds, where it was jerked up short in its fall by the opening chute. As I circled the chute the German clasped his hands over his head, and shook them as if to tell me he was OK. I narrowly missed colliding with the burning debris of the ME-109 as it finally lost momentum and came spinning toward the ground from out of the clouds. I dispatched the rest of my flight back to patrol duty, but I stayed to circle the German pilot in his descent to earth, where I figured he would probably be captured by the English troops around Caen. There were still a lot of Spitfires buzzing around, and I had heard that some of the English pilots who had survived the Battle of Britain were inclined to be pretty bitter about allowing German pilots safe descent after bail out. Personally, I gave little credence to this rumor, but since I was responsible for the poor devil's being in this predicament, I decided it was the least I could do to give him a fighting chance to survive, as he was no longer a threat to invasion operations. Besides, he quite possibly might have valuable information for the interrogation people. At any rate, I knew if our positions were reversed, I would appreciate similar treatment from a German. So I continued to fly around the pilot as he floated down to the outskirts of Caen, where I could see English troops rushing to the probable landing area.

There was one anxious moment, as I circled lower. The Tommies had pointed their guns at me, evidently mistaking my Mustang for an ME-109, but by violently rocking my wings, I was able to convince most of them that I was an ally, and they lowered their arms. I didn't stick around long to find out whether or not they were fully convinced. I had a feeling I had carried compassion for the German far enough. After I rejoined the patrol, we took a few more sweeps of the beachhead, and then returned to base after the relief patrol arrived.

I had watched the ME-109 crash into a wooded area near a château far to the west toward our base at Strip A-2. In the plunge earthward, the fire must have been snuffed out, for the ME-109 volplaned at the last moment from its tight spin into a shallow gliding crash which produced no visible fire or smoke. Mentally making a note of the location of the crash, since it seemed to be within twenty miles of our strip, I resolved to get a jeep and examine the wreckage, and perhaps cut a swastika from it for a souvenir. After debriefing, I got my crew chief, Tommy, and we set out on the road to Bayeux and Caen. Sure enough, I found the château, behind which was a wooded area in which we found the 109 more or less intact. From the wing root to the nose of the plane we counted around two hundred 50-caliber holes. No wonder the pilot had bailed out so quickly! I knew that I had scored a number of hits, but I had no idea that the fire had been so concentrated. It gave me a new and added respect for the destructive powers of my guns. Tommy cut a swastika from the vertical stabilizer for me, collecting various other relics for himself, and we returned to base. Our hopes for air combat were revived somewhat, for this incident proved the Luftwaffe was still in business—which we were beginning to doubt, having seen so little of them since the invasion. There is nothing like a good air fight to keep fighter pilots on their toes and eager to go.

My next patrol took place on June 30. This time it was to the south in the Vire-Caen area, and again Lady Luck smiled upon me, providing another encounter with the enemy. The weather was good with only a suggestion of cirrus clouds at high altitude. Climbing out from the strip toward Vire with my two flights, I saw what appeared to be bogies at twelve o'clock high and approximately 30,000 feet. Going to maximum climb and flipping on gun and sight switches, I informed the flight of the bogies' location, and gave chase. We seemed to be closing well from the rear. We were making a perfect blind approach. After ten or fifteen minutes of climbing we reached their altitude about a thousand yards behind them, and we recognized them as a flight of ME-109s flying to the south. Hoping that they wouldn't see us creeping up on them, I kept pressing on to get within good range, telling my flights to keep closed in tight until we were in range.

As I closed in, I sighted on the 109 to the left of the formation, leaving the others for my flights to pick up. I put the pip right on his tail and fired off a burst. The range was deceptive at this high altitude, and the tracers dropped away under the aircraft without scoring a strike. Naturally, the other 109s saw the fire, and broke to the right with my Mustangs hot on their tails. For some inexplicable reason my target kept right on course without breaking, so I raised the pip to just over his rudder top, and fired another long burst. This time multiple strikes blossomed all over the plane causing it to stream volumes of black smoke. I couldn't see any visible flame, and the pilot didn't bail out, so I pressed in for another attack as he began a slow descent. I scored another cluster of strikes, and the smoke increased as he wobbled into a turn to the left, still losing altitude. Now I realized why there had been no flame. We were at an altitude of 25,000 feet, and there wasn't enough oxygen at this height to support a freely burning fire. On the chance the plane might still be flyable, I fired again, hitting the whole length of his wingspan and fuselage. The 109 yawed wildly from the impact, and cartwheeled over into a vertical plunge. As he hit the lower altitudes, the black smoke turned to a cloud of bright yellow flames which soon enveloped the entire craft.

Suddenly I saw tracers flash past me on the right, closely followed by two ME-109s traveling at great speed, who were obviously about to overrun me. Dropping downward in a following trajectory, I fired a burst at the leader's flight path missing him, but managing to hit his wingman as he followed the leader through my line of fire. The leader continued his dive for the deck, but his wingman straightened out ahead of me, evidently somewhat damaged by my chance hits. I let the leader go, and followed the wingman. I closed to close range to finish him off. Intent on completing this job, I held fire until I was sure I was in range, and then poured fire from all six guns. He blew apart instantly. I turned in search of my patrol mates wondering fleetingly if I wasn't getting a little bit flak happy. I joined the flight, and we proceeded with the patrol for a while before returning to base.

CHAPTER 9

For the next three days I flew no missions, letting my flight leaders take over the lead while I cleared up ever-present organizational problems of the squadron on the ground. On the afternoon of July 3 I was summoned to Group Headquarters where the Group Commander, Colonel Bickell, informed me that on the Fourth of July, General Elwood R. Quesada would arrive with the Commander-in-Chief of the Allied invasion forces, General Dwight D. Eisenhower. They would fly a personal reconnaissance of the Saint-Lô area in the twin-seated Mustang. The craft mentioned was an old war-weary fighter we had modified by removing the fuselage fuel tank from behind the pilot, putting in its place a second seat. We used this plane occasionally to demonstrate tactics to new pilots, and to give rides to our crew chiefs. Colonel Bickell informed me that he had chosen my squadron to provide the other three aircraft and pilots for protective escort to the two generals during their flight over the area. I was extremely proud to have my squadron chosen to accompany such important personnel, though I must admit, the grave responsibility made me a little nervous.

I hurried back to set up the mission for the next day with engineering and operations. Together with my engineering officer, Lieutenant Bernard Ginsberg, his line chief, Master Sergeant Josiah Belden, and my operations officer, Captain Verlin Chambers, I selected my aircraft and crews. I selected the pilots from my senior flight commanders. General Quesada would lead the flight, with a flight commander who had flown over fifty missions on his wing, and I would lead the second element with another flight commander on my wing. The three accompanying pilots would have a cumulative experience of some 175 missions and forty aerial victories. Saint-Lô and the front lines were no more than twelve miles from the strip, so the mission shouldn't last more than about half-an-hour. There would be other Group aircraft deployed on routine missions nearby, who would be briefed to converge on the recon flight if unforeseen enemy aircraft activity developed in the area. The plan was to carry out the flight under the guise of a routine patrol flight, and to have nothing said over the RT that would give the slightest indication this was a special flight or that important personnel were involved. If anything happened to that old war-weary Mustang and its important passengers, the Allied troops would be dealt a crippling psychological blow. Needless to say, I slept fitfully that night.

The next morning as I looked over the twin-seater, I couldn't help but wonder if General Eisenhower would know that when he climbed into the back seat he would virtually be trapped there until landing when the crew chief could unfasten the closures. It would have been a near impossibility to get out of that rear seat in the air. I myself wouldn't have ridden in the back seat of that monster for all the tea in China. The other planes I had chosen were ready, but Sergeant Belden asked me if I would use a brand-new P-51D that his boys had been working on all night. While I was reluctant to fly any plane but my own, I didn't wish to seem unappreciative of the crew's hard work, and agreed to fly the 51. I had reason later to wish I hadn't.

At briefing my pilots and I were introduced to General Eisenhower who shook each of us by the hand, saying that he understood that he was to be flying with the finest fighter pilots in the ETO. It was deeply gratifying to be so addressed by the Supreme Commander of the Allied Forces. The general seemed genuinely interested in us and in our opinions. He was a man of authority and determination, whose manner impressed all those who saw him.

As we went to our planes, I watched General Eisenhower climb with some difficulty through the small opening behind the cockpit into the cramped bucket seat. There wasn't enough room for both him and a parachute, so the general flew without one. I watched his face as the crew chief buttoned down the Zeus fasteners on the Plexiglas window with a screwdriver, and if he had any misgivings about his obvious helplessness, he showed no concern.

I manned the brand-new Mustang, and started the engine. At the end of the runway General Quesada took off with his wingman in formation, and after a quick three-count I gave it the gas and followed with my wingman. Breaking ground, I pulled up the gear and started milking up the flaps. We caught the leading element within a mile of the strip, and settled into tactical combat formation on the general's right side. After we had climbed to 5000 feet, I made a visual post-take-off check of the cockpit, which I had neglected to do earlier, so preoccupied had I been with seeing that the other planes had gotten off safely. It was then I noticed that something was wrong. The oil-pressure gauge was stopped at zero, and not a quiver of the needle indicated any lubrication of the engine. I knew that without lubrication I had about five minutes' flying time before the engine would catch fire. I had visions of the horde of German fighters which would flock to the area at the first signs of flame, and I knew I had to get out of the area as quickly as possible. I didn't dare announce my departure over the RT, the Germans were constantly tuned in to our radio communications. In desperation I waved off my wingman and closed up to the general's plane. As I caught General Quesada's eye, I pointed at my engine nose and gave the cut engine hand signal. The general gave a quick nod, and without waiting for further acknowledgment I peeled away from the flight in a 180-degree turn. After leveling-off I shoved the nose down in a dive for the strip, cutting my rpm's to reduce the friction which must be building up terrific heat.

I hoped the others would not interpret my abrupt departure as a warning of attack, and wondered what I'd do if the engine packed up before I reached the strip. I was loath to damage a brand-new plane. The temperature gauge showed a quite normal reading, which surprised me since the oil-pressure needle still hung lifeless at zero. I saw the strip coming up and came straight into the runway under reduced power, cutting the throttle even before I touched down in an attempt to save the engine. Rolling to a stop halfway down the runway, I cut the switch and turned off the transmitter.

I climbed out of the plane as they came to tow it away, and walked to squadron operations to wait for a report on the aircraft. After a while Sergeant Belden came in looking very embarrassed. It seems that the new plane had been in perfect condition except for a disconnected pressure-sensing line which accounted for the zero reading I got on the oil gauge. Fortunately no real harm was done, and I told Sergeant Belden not to worry about the incident, sending him back to the line. Personally, I was very upset at having to leave the mission under such circumstances, and swore never again to fly any plane but my own.

Soon the recon flight returned, and I rushed out to the hardstand of the twin-seater. As I arrived General Eisenhower was being helped out of his cubbyhole with a wide grin on his face. He was so pleased with the mission that he could hardly wait to get back to his planning staff and start the gears grinding. I went up to General Quesada to apologize for my sudden departure and explain the reasons for it. The general, much to my relief, understood the dilemma, and approved of my action in the face of it. Although it was consoling to receive official sanction, I still felt a little foolish in light of the nature of the false alarm. But, of course, I had no way of determining this at the time.

This was the first time in history that a ground general had personally reconnoitered the terrain of a planned battle operation from a fighter aircraft in the presence of the enemy. Toward the end of July we took part in this operation which became known as "the breakthrough at Saint-Lô." In these operations General George S. Patton and his famed Third Army made the dramatic gains on enemy territory. Their advance was not halted until the supply line was weakened by distance before the defenses of Metz.

On July 30, during the Saint-Lô breakthrough, I led another patrol south to the Vire area, with some hope of contacting enemy aircraft. The weather was generally good, but there was a low scattered cloud covering at about five or six thousand feet. The Germans loved to operate in such conditions, because the clouds provided them a good hiding place. This encouraged my feeling that there was a good possibility contacting some of the by now scarce Luftwaffe. I took off with two flights and climbed to 30,000 feet, my intended patrol altitude on the south leg to Vire. I couldn't see a blessed thing in the sky and sighed in resignation, thinking we were doomed to another boring milkrun.

We were almost to the southern limits of our patrol area when I thought I saw a single bogie at twelve o'clock. Alerting the flight I increased power and prop to combat settings, and switched on the guns and sight. With increased speed we crept up on the bogie, which was soon identifiable as an ME-109. As we drew closer he began a slow shallow turn to the left toward the interior of France. I pushed my engine controls to the limit, determined to catch the 109 before he could go for the cloud cover below. The rest of my boys weren't so eager to punish their engines, and they drifted behind me, content to protect my rear as I pursued the German. I cut inside his turning radius, and came within long-range firing distance. We were fairly evenly matched in speed, and it became more difficult to overtake him. I estimated the range and let fly with a test burst. Toward the end of the burst I got one lonely strike in the vicinity of his cockpit which seemed to slow him down a bit, as he increased his diving angle. I was pleased at this for I knew I could overtake him in a dive. I chased him for the next few minutes, edging closer and closer. Firing intermittently, I was able to get a scattering of strikes which continued to slow him down. Just before he reached the cloud deck I hit him with a solid burst of 50s which caused the plane to belch a huge ball of fire. I almost collided with his canopy which flew back at me as the pilot bailed out of the burning craft.

I pulled up into a climb to pick up my flight, and we continued our patrol, searching unsuccessfully for more enemy aircraft. After two and a half hours we returned to base. Ninety-nine percent of the time we landed from the north because of the prevailing offshore wind at Strip A-2, and for the past week I had noticed a lot of Army ground activity just south of the strip. I had never paid particular attention to what they had been doing, but today as we landed I glanced down as I turned into the approach, and was shocked at what I saw. It was a grim scene. There, laid out in neat, multiple rows, were hundreds of dead GIs, victims of the voracious maw of ground combat. The scene brought home with shocking force the high price the ground forces were paying for real-estate in the invasion. It wasn't a sight to inspire confidence, and I worried about the effect it might have on the morale of my pilots, who were forced to see it every time they came in for a landing.

CHAPTER 10

For two months my pilots had been flying twice-daily missions without any leave or time off for recreation. This concentrated effort didn't phase the old hands, but we worried about the newer replacement pilots. A continuous diet of combat without recreational opportunity as a safety release for their emotions was a lot to ask of them. One day a few of the veteran pilots suggested that we throw a squadron party and I quickly agreed, requesting from Group a twenty-four-hour stand-down for my squadron. We were granted the time, and proceeded with plans for the party. The contents of our whisky larder amounted to ten or twelve bottles, which boded ill for the conviviality of our party. But Captain "Doc" Richard N. O'Dell, our squadron flight surgeon, came to our aid, providing several gallons of good grain alcohol with which we multiplied the existing stock to about three or four times its original volume. So the booze supply was both adequate and potent. Captain Max Lamb and some of the other old pros had discovered that a nearby field hospital unit by happy circumstance happened by merest chance to have some 20 to 30 nurses assigned to it. An invitation was dispatched to all nurses not on duty the night of our festivities, and was promptly accepted. The enlisted men volunteered to supply bartenders and a musical combo, and surprised us by building a circus tent out of old parachutes, with a wooden floor and a magnificent bar at the far end. All this was done overnight without our knowing it. I assigned jeeps from the squadron motor pool to transport the nurses, and had the Officers' Mess supply a fine array of buffet delicacies bartered from the local citizenry.

The party got off with a bang, as we required everyone attending to quaff down a French Seventy-five to gain admittance. Our version of the drink was half cognac and half champagne. I'm afraid I was a victim of my own elaborate preparations, for I can't even remember when I toddled off to my tent and sank into blessed oblivion. The first indication I had that the evening had been a huge success was when Captain Fred Hageman, my Squadron Exec. woke me up to report Captain Bob Goodnight and Lieutenant Charles Simonson were missing with two jeeps. I staggered through a cold shower, hurried to my office, where the mystery had already been solved over the field phone.

It seemed that Bob Goodnight had decided to borrow a jeep to escort one of the nurses back to the field hospital. It was around 3 A.M., and there was nothing but convoy light to guide him, which was comparable to using a firefly for a lantern in a coal mine. It just so happened that Lieutenant Simonson had conceived of the same brilliant idea about twenty minutes earlier, and as Goodnight was approaching the field hospital, Simonson was starting back. Like well trained pilots they zeroed in nose to nose at about fifteen mph! Fortunately, the nurse was in a very relaxed condition and suffered no more than the indignity of being rudely awakened as she rolled unceremoniously into the weeds. Simonson was bruised, but relatively undamaged. Poor old Bob, bleary eyed but intent upon his vast responsibilities, was hunched down over the steering wheel, peering intently through the spokes, and received a broken jaw for his gallantry. The next morning we found them both patients at the hospital, one painted with iodine for his bruises, and the other with his teeth wired together. It was all hilariously funny until we learned that we were to lose Bob Goodnight on a transfer back to England where he was to be treated for the broken jaw. I was sad to see him go, for we had been together since our flight school days, and it was like parting with a brother. At least I had the consolation of knowing he was safe and would survive the war.

After a mission on the 30th of July, on which I was lucky enough to shoot down a 109, I flew seven more missions, most of which were routine milkruns.

The only exception was the mission of August 3. We had been assigned to escort a group of B-26 bombers to a target northwest of Paris through huge clouds at medium altitude. Although we had no enemy aircraft to contend with, the German flak gave everyone a rough time. On the target run, I was watching the B-26s drop their explosives, when I saw one of them receive a direct hit in the bombardier's section, and spin out of control for a few thousand feet. Surprisingly he recovered at low altitude, and began flying a straight course again.

The only trouble was that his course was now to the northeast, toward Germany. I took my flight and dove alongside the bomber, calling the pilot on "B" channel to ask if his ship was all right and where he was going. After a few seconds I got the answer that the bomber answered its controls but that all instruments were gone including his compass. Everyone on the ship was wounded except him; his bombardier was missing, along with the nose of his ship and there was a 200 mph gale rushing through the aircraft; he didn't have the slightest idea which way to fly for home after the spin. Otherwise he was all right. He asked that we point out the direction of the beachhead, where he would try a crash landing. Impressed with the pilot's courage I told him we would do better than that. We throttled down to his speed so that he could follow us and led him to a newly constructed bomber strip near Bayeaux, made expressly for his kind of emergency. After an hour of flight we were over the special field and the bomber pilot told me his airspeed indicator was gone, and that he didn't dare land without one. On top of that he couldn't bail out because he had wounded men aboard who would be unable to jump.

I called my flight to tell them to circuit the field for a few minutes. Then I called the bomber pilot, and told him to lower his wheels and flaps, and to fly close formation on me. After we both were squared away I asked him at what speed he wanted to land. He replied that if I could get him over the fence at 120 mph he could make it from there. I acknowledged and we made an overhead 360-degree pattern while I sang out our dropping airspeed on the radio. It worked like a charm. I was careful to make a big wide pattern to keep the turns gentle enough for him to stay with me, and took him in at the south end of the runway at 20′ altitude and 115 mph. Here I pulled up to the left raising my gear and flaps as I watched him cut power to touch down like a feather. His brakes must have been gone as well as everything else, for he rolled the entire length of the strip before stopping. I wagged my wings and peeled off to join my waiting flight to return to Strip A-2.

On the afternoon of August 7 following a fruitless morning mission I took off with the squadron for a sweep of the area of Chartres. We had hit the regular airfields used by the Germans so much that they were abandoning them for open fields, highways or almost any level area close to forests which would provide camouflage. In the briefing I had made a point of discussing these hidden makeshift airdromes. It had been a while since we had been able to find any of the enemy aloft. And we determined to seek them on the ground.

We were at 10,000 feet when we arrived over our landmark, the famous thirteenth-century Gothic cathedral of Chartres. I turned east following a wide straight highway, inspecting its adjoining fields and forests for evidence of clandestine Luftwaffe activity. After approximately ten miles of cruising I saw a suspicious collection of objects at the east end of a huge field bounded on two sides by woods. I approached the location for a closer look. When I descended to about 3000 feet I could see that the objects were wheat sheaves, but I could also detect the familiar outlines of an ME-109 peeking from beneath. I called my discovery to the squadron and made a firing pass on the hidden 109, getting an excellent pattern of strikes, and it exploded and burned. I pulled up and over, going for the fringe of forest where others in the squadron had discovered more fighters parked. For the next five minutes we gave the concealed airdrome a good working over. As far as we could see there was no returning ground fire, but the Germans must have been using bullets without tracers, for near the end of our strafing I heard one of my pilots exclaim that his plane had been hit in the engine, and was losing power. I identified the pilot as Lieutenant Charles Simonson, and told his wingman to escort him back toward the beachhead immediately. The two of them left on a westerly course, with Simonson's Mustang trailing a thin ribbon of vapor. Praying that he would make it back over the line before his engine died, I collected the rest of the squadron, and headed after them. Before we could overtake them I heard Simonson announce that he was going to bail out before his aircraft caught fire. A minute later I heard his wingman urging him to hurry and leave the Mustang before he got too low; then there was silence over the RT.

Impatiently I queried the wingman. Had Simonson jumped, and if so, had he made it down OK? After a moment's pause the voice of the wingman cut in informing us that Simonson had jumped, his chute had opened, and that he had landed in the midst of a battalion of American tanks. Simonson was now clambering on one of them to hitch a ride back to our lines. The squadron perked up at hearing this welcome news, and we happily returned to our beachhead strip for landing. As we flew I tallied up the reported number of ME-109s destroyed by each pilot. The total came to at least nineteen, which made the mission a resounding success, particularly in view of our getting Simonson back unharmed.

We moved our base of operations once again during the 11th through the 13th of August, from the A-2 beach strip to a field near Montfort. The new airdrome was about 25 miles west of Rennes at the root of the Brest Peninsula, and we were curious to see it since the base had been recently held by the Luftwaffe before Patton's rapid advance had forced them to flee. It was interestingly situated with pockets of German resistance all around it, bypassed by the fast-moving Third Army. To the west of us a large fortification was still manned by a diehard German regiment. There was a pocket of Germans still offering resistance south, at Saint-Nazaire, and another around Fallais in the east. All this gave the new base an unexpected atmosphere of tension. But when we arrived we found the landing strip was in good shape, although the buildings were severely damaged. Group Command promptly appropriated the buildings for its own use, and the squadrons set up bivouac areas in tents again as before.

One thing that provided a bit of humor was the fuel we used for our pot-bellied stoves. We had found chunks of a yellow cake-like substance scattered all over the base, and it wasn't long before some clever GI discovered that the stuff burned readily in our tent stoves. Everyone used the magic fuel freely until one day a visiting ordnance officer identified the yellow chunks as high explosive jelly that had evidently been scattered about when the Luftwaffe destroyed their bomb dump before retreating. At that news our source of free heat came to an end in a hurry.

From the 14th through the 18th of August I flew five patrols over eastern France during which we strafed German road columns, hoping to impair the flexibility of the German High Command who was desperately trying to halt the American advance. During this period we would get heavy ground fire when occasionally bad weather conditions forced us low over the Fallais Gap area as we felt our way to the base. It was during one of these barrages that I collected a hole in my wing which was to be the second and last time I was hit by ground fire.

On the 26th of August I took another patrol of my squadron to Reims, and we surprised the airdrome at Beauvais during refueling operations. I took my whole outfit in on a pass, and clobbered all the FW-190s visible. Pulling up to the left in a circle of the field I saw an undamaged 190 sitting in front of a hangar, so I called for one more pass over the field. Ducking down to twenty feet above the deck I came in withholding my fire until close range. When I tripped the trigger the FW-190 exploded, creating a fire which poured into the hangar and engulfed the planes within. By now heavy ground fire had developed threatening to pick off someone of my patrol, and I liked the odds we already had—about fifteen to nothing—and I wanted it to stay that way, so I ordered everyone to leave the area for rendezvous ten miles west. I collected my squadron at the rendezvous point, and found all Mustangs were present and accounted for. Pleased at the squadron's brilliant success I set course for our base, little realizing that I had destroyed my last German plane of the war.

On the morning of September 5, I got a hurried call from group. A few minutes after arriving at Group Headquarters I was told by the Army Liaison Officer of a gun position in the German coastal fort at Brest. The Army was attacking this isolated pocket, but this particular gun couldn't be touched by mortar fire or field guns and was holding up the attack. It had to be neutralized quick, and Group wanted us to do it by dive-bombing. The gun emplacement was in an inner line of defense, and was protected by a cliff-like projection. I felt we could use a shallow trajectory with explosives and napalm with good results. Back at squadron operations I set up the mission with eight aircraft manned by experienced pilots whom I briefed in detail and within thirty minutes we were in the air. My lead flight had eight 500-pound bombs, and the second flight had eight tanks of napalm. I planned to take the high explosives in first with skip-bombing technique, and to follow this up immediately with the napalm.

It was less than a half-hour's flying before we arrived over the target area, and after circling for four or five minutes I located the emplacement, and selected our attack course. I chose a path at about 500 feet which took us over a small hill before we got to the emplacement. The hill might give some protection from ground fire. I put the two flights in line astern for concentrated bombing, and peeled off about a mile out from the target with the seven other Mustangs following. Halfway down I heard one of the boys cry over the RT, "My God, look what's coming from above!" Craning my head I looked up and saw an entire group of B-26s directly overhead with their bomb bays wide open. No one had told me about the bombers being here, but now it was too late to abort the mission, and the Army said it was a priority-one target of the utmost urgency. I continued my dive for the gun emplacement, hoping we could get out of there be-

28. My last Mustang was named "Short-Fuse" because Sallee had married somebody else during my absence! Here I am early in my second tour with my ground crew. S/Sgt. C. H. Thompson, on the left, kept all my Mustangs in tip-top condition.

29. Lt. Col. "Turk" Teschner, with whom I had an eventful ride to Chartres by car.

30. "Turk" and I saw this FW-190 and many others we'd shot down on our trip to Chartres.

31. Proof of the saying "There are old pilots and bold pilots, but no old–bold pilots." A mini-reunion of the 354th F.G. at Randolph Field in 1972. Left to right: Jack Bradley, Ken Martin, myself, Clayton Gross and Kenny Dahlberg.

32. My short tour with the Fourth Fighter Wing in Korea lasted from December 1951 to March 1952. This photo was taken after returning to Kimpo Air Base on a search mission; the last 90 miles in a powerless glide. I found the F-86A slipped like a lady in a dead-stick landing.

fore the B-26s dropped. If one of their bombs exploded below us at this altitude it would literally blow our wings off. The emplacement was dead ahead, and I headed straight for it trimming the ship to fly as straight and level as possible. Just as the emplacement disappeared under my nose I released my own bombs and peeled up for altitude. Watching behind my tail as I climbed I saw my bombs burst on target, a good lucky hit.

My flights had closed up their intervals, and their bombs and napalm tanks hit in such quick succession that it looked as if they were spit out of a machine gun. The target was plastered with the best series of hits I had ever seen. Each one of my Mustangs got out of the mess without a scratch, though bombs from the B-26 Group had begun to fall all around us before the last two or three fighters pulled up and away. As my boys finished their run my heart almost stopped for fear I'd killed one of my friends by not aborting the mission. But with a flush of pure joy I saw the last of them climbing up from the cloud of boiling dust as if the very devil himself were on their tail.

We felt so good about the results of our run and our good luck in escaping the rain of bombs from above that we formed up again and went up to give escort to the bombers. Returning to base we were told that the Army had described our mission as "highly successful" and had been able to proceed with their attack without further hindrance from the once impregnable gun.

CHAPTER 11

The day after the napalm mission to Brest I was called to the Group Commander's office where I found Colonel Bickell with Major Jack Bradley, the CO of the 353rd Squadron. Colonel Bickell hedged with small talk for a few minutes and then threw us some block-busting information.

It seems that Ninth Air Force had at last gotten around to checking up on the combat hours and missions flown by our personnel, and had decided that it was time that both Jack and I were grounded from further combat since we both had surpassed the official quota. Colonel Bickell further explained that he was instructed to send one of us back to the U.S. immediately on Rest and Return. Jack and I had identical seniority, and the colonel was having difficulty deciding which of us to send. I had over 294 hours combat time with ninety-six missions under my belt, but Jack had approximately the same, and Colonel Bickell at length asked that we decide between ourselves which should go and which should stay. I spoke up briskly, pointing out that Jack was married with a family, whereas I was still single, and that as far as I was concerned this decided the point. Jack demurred, but

Colonel Bickell and I finally convinced him that it was only fair to his wife and family that he return at this opportunity. Endeavoring to put Jack at his ease I told him that I wasn't ready to stop flying combat just now anyway, and that I reckoned there were a few more victories with my name on them I had not yet collected.

At this flippant remark Colonel Bickell told me regretfully that my combat flying was over, for even though I would stay with the Group in command of the 356th Squadron, orders from higher headquarters were that I should be denied exposure to combat. I could spend the remaining time I had with the squadron choosing a successor as commanding officer, but soon I, too, was to be sent home. At this point I interposed that I knew already who my successor should be: Frank O'Connor. If I were not able to lead the squadron in combat, I felt, he should assume command immediately, and I would be privileged to serve under him in any capacity while awaiting further orders. Colonel Bickell knew that O'Connor had been my second-in-command for many months, and that I considered him my co-commander rather than my subordinate, so the issue was resolved then and there.

A dividend of our squadron's exceptionally low loss record was that I had many able and seasoned officers capable of leading a squadron. It was disheartening for me to know I would never again fly with the 356th; yet the opportunity to give the command to my close friend Frank O'Connor, who so strongly deserved the distinction, allayed my sadness and nostalgia. The squadron couldn't be in better hands than those of Frank O'Connor.

With nothing better to do, for the next few days, I sat down with the squadron operational records to review my total combat tour. From December 1, 1943, to September 5, 1944, I had flown 96 combat missions while spending 294 hours and 40 minutes in the air. I had submitted claims for 32½ enemy aircraft destroyed. Of these 32½ destroyed enemy aircraft, 20 were aerial victories and 12½ were destroyed as a result of strafing.

The only injuries that I had incurred were connected with two combat related incidents. When I shot down an ME-109 over Brunswick, Germany, on the 30th of January I was so close to him when he exploded that I instinctively ducked my head in the cockpit, and had hit my mouth on the cowling, fracturing a front tooth. The tooth came to throb distractingly at high altitude, and finally had to be extracted. But that was the end of that. Then following the mission on April 11, I landed at Boxsted after descending through a reverse inversion which had coated my wings with a thin layer of ice. I had shot down two German aircraft, and I was in a hurry to tell Tommy, my crew chief, about them. I jumped out of the cockpit, and slipped off the wing to the ground. The fall hurt my back, but it seemed to recover in time. Ten years later, however, while flying Saber jet fighters in Korea the back injury returned, developing into an arthritic condition which caused my eventual retirement from the Air Force.

On the 17th of September the group moved from Montfort in Brittany to Orconte, another advanced strip a few miles west of Saint-Dizier. I had turned the squadron over to Frank, and had no duties to perform so I requested permission from Colonel Bickell to move to the new base by jeep. I wanted to see some of the French countryside over which we had fought so painfully to recover, and in addition to check the results of our recent strafing attacks on the hidden airfields west of Chartres. Colonel Bickell approved my plan enthusiastically. Lieutenant Colonel Charles Teschner was also waiting for transfer orders for home and I talked him into going with me on my little tour. "Turk" Teschner had joined the group while we were at Maidstone; Lieutenant Colonel Wally Mace, our former Deputy Group CO, had been transferred to higher headquarters, and Turk had come to us from another unit to take his place. Turk and I had become good friends in the intervening months, and it was good to have a buddy along to share the trip. We planned to take two days, with an overnight stopover at a hospital unit stationed at Chartres.

We left early one bright sunny day with our duffel bags and a few snacks in the jeep. Turk and I were in our dress uniforms, with our leather flight jackets for comfortable traveling. Since the country we would be going through had been liberated only recently, I wore my .45-caliber automatic under my jacket, and Turk showed up carrying a carbine, which he stashed under the duffels on the rear seat. I asked him if he planned to go deer hunting and he solemnly told me that if we ran into any Wehrmacht stragglers with ideas of capturing two stupid American flying officers he wanted to be able to argue with some kind of authority besides that given to him by Congress. When he learned I was packing a .45 he asked me the embarrassing question: Can you hit anything with it? I admitted that on a good day, with luck, I could probably hit a barn at ten paces, and on this note we piled into the jeep and took off in a cloud of dust.

About every hour we would come upon a rustic building which resembled some sort of countryside pub, and being traditionally curious pilots, stopped to investigate each of them. Nine times out of ten we would indeed find a quaint and fully equipped French inn. In spite of the war these staunch Gallic institutions were open and ready to do business, and we were happy to oblige. Our stops usually ended with us buying drinks for every Frenchman from five miles around. They appeared as if by magic when the word went out that two Americans were at the local grog hall buying wine as if it were going out of style. Since I was driving over strange roads I drank mostly cider, but Turk, the passenger, could participate more fully in the festive atmosphere generated by Frenchmen who insisted on toasting us as the liberators of all France.

By late in the afternoon we were well along toward Chartres. I had cider coming out of my ears, and old Turk was in high gear. Everything was rosy, and we were having a wonderful time cruising along the country lane toward Chartres.

After a while Turk climbed into the back of the jeep, and, with a bottle of gin from his duffel in one hand and his carbine in the other, announced that he was going to ride shotgun for the rest of the trip. Laughing at the scene we presented I turned back to my driving thinking it wouldn't be long before Turk would fall asleep.

A few minutes later I almost fell out of the car as Turk suddenly roared in my ear, "Stop the jeep, Dick! There's a German out in the middle of that field, and I'm going to shoot the SOB!" Startled, I slammed on the brakes, and Turk tumbled head-first into the front seat beside me. I looked warily out into the adjacent field, and saw an old French farmer wearily plodding behind his horse and plow. There was no one in sight but the farmer, who was unaware of us.

"Turk, you crazy galoot. That's no German. That's a French farmer plowing his field."

"The hell you say! That's a German for sure, and I'm going to shoot him!" Turk yelled. Reaching across the seat I groped for the carbine, and jerked it forcibly out of his hands. Turk sprawled back into the rear seat, looking at me as if I had lost my mind. "You'd better quit horsing around, Dick, or you'll get us both clobbered by those damned Germans," he said sadly, lying on his back.

I tried to convince him that it was a genuine Frenchman that he had seen, but he wouldn't be persuaded, and we argued like a couple of fishmongers until Turk passed out in midsentence. He had enjoyed one toast too many, thank the Lord! Checking the carbine I found to my relief that it was empty of shells, and I hid it under my seat. Still trembling from the tension this whole mad incident had created, I drove on toward Chartres. I relaxed as the humorous aspect hit me, and I couldn't help laughing out loud as I drove, causing Frenchmen to stop and stare at us, wondering, no doubt, what the crazy Americans were doing that was so funny.

I reached the city of Chartres at twilight, and made my way along its streets toward the cathedral spires. Near the cathedral was a Hospital Unit where we hoped to cadge overnight accommodations. Arriving at the cathedral I found the Hospital Unit and was pleased to learn we would be welcome to quarter overnight in what they called "rectory quarters" at the cathedral itself. In jig time I established Turk and myself in the quarters offered, and we spent most of the next hour rejoining reality with the help of a much-needed shower. Finally, sober and famished, we joined the hospital staff at supper mess where we divided our time between eating and trying to date the nurses. The only success I had was in eating, so I wandered back to our room, and climbed into my sack where I fell asleep pondering the best way to locate the German airdome that my squadron and I had so lately demolished.

The next morning I woke up raring to go, much to the disgust of Turk who evidently had been more fortunate than I the preceding evening. With spiteful glee I rolled him out of the sack and badgered him into getting dressed for breakfast. After eating we thanked the hospital personnel for their hospitality, and prepared to depart.

I was already in the jeep with the motor running, but Turk was still rummaging around in our sleeping quarters. Impatiently I yelled for Turk to hurry up and he came to the door, proclaiming that some one had stolen his carbine. I reached under the seat and produced the gun, with the remark that it probably would have been a good thing if some one *had* stolen it since we were bound to come across more innocent French farmers in the course of the day. Turk looked puzzled and demanded to know what the hell French farmers had to do with it. He didn't even remember our fiasco of yesterday, and furthermore he wouldn't believe me when I told him about it. Laughing and needling Turk about the difference between farmers and Germans I drove to the east of Chartres where I found a long straight road leading to the area we sought.

After ten or twelve miles we saw wrecked hangars in

the woods to our left, and we drove cautiously toward them. Inside the wreckage of the hangars we found remains of French Moran fighters, FW-190s, ME-109s and other smaller craft. We spent an hour inspecting and photographing the debris. It was a bit puzzling to me, for I couldn't remember hitting anything with the squadron on this side of the road. I remembered distinctly that our strafing had been to the south of the road coming from Chartres, and finally concluded that the site where we were must have been a secret engineering depot hidden apart from the flying field that we clobbered. It must have been hit by someone else after we had stumbled over the neighboring flying field. We returned to the road, and drove a little way farther until we came upon a huge open field bordered by woods on the south and west. I recognized it immediately, and drove to the east end of the field where I had made my initial attack. A mile and a half later we found it and I had been correct. It was a ME-109, and my APIs had burned it to a crisp. In the surrounding trees we found more Me-109s in various degrees of destruction, none of them repairable. At least twenty wrecks were tucked into camouflaged hardstands. Scattered around the area were charred vehicles, and pits easily recognizable as antiaircraft emplacements (although no armament pieces now rested on the empty swivel posts). The devastated German airdrome was interesting to inspect but it gave me an eerie feeling to realize that not long ago it was a bustling center inhabited by enemy personnel and not much different from ourselves. I felt a twinge of compassion for the pilots who must have watched the destruction of their irreplaceable fighting planes. Pilots come as close as anyone can to love and affection for an inanimate machine; when airborne their machine becomes a vibrant creature which transmits power. Pilots of all nationalities share a common respect for their companion in combat, the fighter plane.

It wasn't long before the depressing scene of the gutted airdrome overcame my curiosity, and I called to Turk who also had seen enough. It was with no sense of victory or jubilation that we slowly and thoughtfully drove away eastward toward our new base. As we proceeded farther toward Saint-Dizier we continually came upon burnt-out tanks and sundry paraphernalia of the retreating Wehrmacht. We naturally stopped and inspected firsthand this flotsam of war, the result of our own action in the first stages of the Invasion. The uncanny immediacy of these scenes put us both on edge and we kept looking into the surrounding fields, half-expecting the German personnel who had manned the ruined equipment to appear at any time. I noticed that Turk kept his carbine slung ready for action, and even I constantly hefted my .45 as we made these periodic stops. Finally after a long day's journey we arrived at the 354th Squadron's new landing strip, A-66.

At the advanced strip I tried for several days to be a helpful non-combatant, but I grew restive at not being allowed to fly with my squadron. I finally requested permission of Colonel Bickell to borrow an L4B liaison aircraft from the 472nd Service Group to fly to Paris for a forty-eight-hour leave. Colonel Bickell was very sympathetic with my predicament and gave his approval, and I quickly got the loan of the L4B from Lieutenant Colonel James M. Sullivan of the service group. I loaded my bags and one Lieutenant Lyle C. Christianson, the assistant group adjutant who also had a leave, into the light plane, and we took off across country for Orly Airport. We spent two relaxed and interesting days in Paris seeing the storied sights, investigating for ourselves the multitude of recreational opportunities offered by this city, the center of Continental taste and custom. After two days we reluctantly tore away from leisure and pleasure and took off from Orly for Strip A-66. After thirty minutes of flying we were comfortably under way, watching the French countryside slide slowly beneath us, and I was intent upon identifying crash sites of past air battles which were to be seen from time to time. I had chosen to fly a course parallel to the Red Ball Highway—so named because of its use by the Transportation Corps for their twenty-four-hour shuttle of Army vehicles supplying the Third Army which had stalled short of Metz. The Air Corps had converted a number of B-24 Liberator bombers into tankers which used a course just north of the Red Ball Highway to fly gasoline to the stalled Third, and I was careful to keep south of the highway to stay safely out of their way.

I had just checked my map to find that we were approximately halfway home when a loud explosion ruptured the smoothness of our flight. Jerking to attention I checked the instruments, and found the tachometer fluttering wildly. Easing back the throttle to soften the loud banging which continued to come from the engine I could feel we were losing power, and I knew that our flying in the little L4B was finished. Yelling to Chris to tighten his seat belt, I started scanning the ground below us for a good spot to set the liaison plane down. The only field

I could safely reach was one just ahead. It was hilly, and to make matters worse, half of the field had been recently plowed. In fact, I could see the farmer still plowing near the spot I had selected for my touchdown. I cut the engine to spare what was left of it, and established my landing glide. Sputtering and backfiring, we must have come within twenty feet of the farmer, but that phlegmatic soul never gave us so much as a fleeting glance. He was either a man of enormous concentration, or he had become completely blasé to airplanes falling out of the sky—having seen so many do so during the war. We touched down without incident, and rolled down the gentle hill to a stop just in front of a hedgerow.

Getting out to inspect the engine, I found that one of the cylinder heads had blown a rocker arm. Temporary repair was impossible and I secured the aircraft by tying the door shut, and pulling a few ignition wires loose in case any meddler should try to start the engine, for I knew we would have to leave it parked there unattended while we hitched a ride to the field via the Red Ball Express. I planned to stop at the first Unit Headquarters I could find to telephone ahead to the Service Group telling them to send a tractor to retrieve their busted bird.

On the hike to the highway we came across the farmer's house in which we found his wife and two youngsters. We couldn't speak French, and they couldn't speak English, but with gestures and charades we explained that we were leaving a plane in their pasture, and that we would be grateful if they made sure no one bothered it. Finally convinced that they understood our request, Chris and I pulled from our bags a mountain of candy, tobacco, and various items that we had bought in Paris, and presented them in thanks to the woman and children. Our near-catastrophe turned into the highlight in our trip as we saw the glow of undisguised pleasure shine and jump in the expressive eyes of the children, who very probably had never seen such treasures throughout the long war years. Both Chris and I felt that we had received far more than we had been privileged to give these sturdy honest folk. We left waving friendly goodbyes to the French family, and proceeded to the highway where we were picked up immediately by a GI driving a truckload of rations.

CHAPTER 12

On November 10, 1944, just before I was flown back to Britain for processing and passage Stateside I received my promotion to lieutenant colonel. There was a little party that night at the Squadron Mess where Colonel Bickell pinned on my silver oak leaves. The occasion was enjoyable, but there were overtones of sadness as I talked to many of my friends and combat colleagues for the last time. I kept scheming to have the orders changed so that I could stay with my outfit; but it was to no avail, and soon I left on my reluctant trip back to the United States. I was sent to Miami Beach, Florida, and installed in a sumptuous hotel suite for fourteen days of "rest and relaxation" while the Air Corps decided upon my next assignment. By now the policy of rest followed by return to your former unit had been stopped, and I had no clue as to where I would next serve. I had decided to quit fighting the system, and had resigned myself to not returning to the ETO and the 356th Fighter Squadron. Miami Beach was the ideal place for leave, but I didn't enjoy the experience much; I couldn't shake my longing to return to my squadron and friends in the ETO.

At last around the 1st of December, I was ordered to

report to the Third Air Force at Tampa. There I reported to General Thomas W. Blackburn, who assigned me to Bartow Air Base, Winter Haven, Florida. At Bartow I was appointed Director of Operations and Training and Deputy CO, and I set about tailoring the training program of the P-51 pilots to include features that I had found essential in combat. One of these items was low level navigation and deck flying technique in which all new pilots seemed to be weak. I immediately designed a course and flying requirement to include this important facet of combat operations, and promptly ran headlong into opposition from headquarters. Being uninitiated in the niceties of Stateside pressure tactics, I immediately fired back a quick, and perhaps impertinent, reply, to the effect that if higher authority would get off its backsides and fly a little combat, it would no doubt realize the crying need for such training—which would free the busy combat units abroad from having to retrain its pilots at the eleventh hour. My vigorous declarations were received coolly, and my superior, Colonel Thompson, who agreed with my evaluation, was caught in the middle. The Third Air Force was concerned with the public reaction to the dangerous implications and the general nuisance of the low-flying aircraft rather than with benefits to the prospective fighter pilots. In others words, "don't rock the boat."

It was my contention that it was much more feasible and realistic to give such training here in the States where mistakes couldn't imperil a mission or other lives, than have it crammed into the already burdened schedule of a unit in combat. For several months we bickered over the subject, but I was given no direct order to drop the subject. With political acumen, Headquarters had no wish to go on record as suppressing something which if given the light of open investigation would prove to have been of merit. So it was that in the Third Air Force I became known as the upstart combat throttle jockey who bid fair to become the proverbial burr under their saddle blanket.

Fed up with the political machinations of Stateside duty, and with what I considered a compromise of my integrity, I wrote directly to General Otto P. Weyland, Commander of the IXXth Tactical Air Command in France, requesting transfer back to my old unit. In a marvelous show of consideration for a former member of his command, General Weyland responded with a personal request to General John H. McCormick of the personnel section of the Pentagon for my reassignment to his command in Europe. It worked like a charm, and I was notified that I was to return immediately to the IXXth Tactical Air Command.

Within a week I was en route to Washington, D.C., where I was to catch an overseas flight to Paris and the headquarters of the Ninth Air Force. As I landed in Washington, the news of imminent cessation of hostilities in Europe caused all travel orders to be canceled, including mine. I went to the transportation officer in charge at the air terminal, and pointed out that my orders represented a personal request from a general officer. The colonel to whom I spoke was impressed enough to get me a staff car, saying that if I could get my orders endorsed at the Pentagon he would gladly get me aboard the first plane available. Arriving at the Pentagon, I started going from one office to another with my problem, beginning with captains and working up through the ranks until finally I was sent into General McCormick himself. After eight frustrating hours of being passed from one office to another, the audience with General McCormick was almost anticlimactic. He listened courteously to my tale of woe and then with a flourish of his hand initialed the orders, and sent me on my way to Paris.

Arriving in Versailles some fifteen hours later, I was pleased to find orders assigning me back to my old Group which was now stationed at Nuremberg, Germany. I was flown to Nuremberg, and upon arrival discovered that Jack Bradley, now a lieutenant colonel, had taken over command of the Group. Jack reassigned me as commanding officer of my old squadron, the 356th, and it was with real pleasure that I prepared to see my old friends once again, but I found out quickly that few of my old pilots were left to greet me. Max Lamb, who was now a major and the Squadron Operations Officer was about the only one left, most of the others having departed on Stateside rotation. Frank O'Connor, whom I had left in charge, had been shot down shortly thereafter.

Max told me the story. It seems that Frank had led a strafing mission, and had led the squadron down on the first pass. As he made his run he discovered a large concentration of flak which he knew would clobber the rest of his boys, and without hesitation he winged over into a headlong attack on the flak emplacements. He accomplished his objective, for he drew the attention of all the guns, and his Mustang was riddled. He was forced to pull up in a zoom, and bail out. The rest of the squadron was saved from devastating fire, but poor old Frank had bought the farm for sure.

He was extremely fortunate in not being hit personally, and had been able to scramble out of his Mustang at the apex of its last climb. He floated down, away from the strafing site, but was seen by German civilians who streamed toward his landing place. As Frank hit the ground he knew that it would be impossible to escape, and judging by the surge of people coming toward him he had a pretty good idea that the only decoration they had in mind was to hang him from the nearest tree. He scrambled out of his parachute harness, and sprinted as if he were Jesse Owens at the 1936 Olympics for a high pile of wood nearby, where he climbed to the top hoping to evade the clutches of the mob for as long as possible. They soon surrounded the woodpile, and although O'Connor couldn't understand German he clearly got the message that they wanted to present him with a wooden cross instead of the Iron Cross. He didn't dare use his .45 which he knew would be powerless to cow so large a mob, and he was beginning to believe the next few seconds would be his last.

At this point he saw a tall individual dressed in a Luftwaffe sergeant's uniform coming toward him unceremoniously shoving and pushing the civilians aside with great rough sweeps of his arms. As the sergeant approached the woodpile the shouts of the mob subsided to a deadly silence. The sergeant stopped at the base of the woodpile, looked disdainfully at the surrounding mob, and turned to Frank atop the pile and said, "Major, please to follow me!" When he said "Major" it sounded like "Ma-yore," but no matter what it sounded like it had the ring of beauty to Frank and he followed closely behind the sergeant who led him away to a waiting vehicle which carried him to captivity for the duration.

The loss of Frank O'Connor in combat was a real blow to the entire Group. His ability, loyalty, and innate personal kindness had endeared him to the men and officers alike of the entire fighter group. I remember the letter I received in the States informing me of his being shot down. I didn't know at the time that he was unhurt and safe, and I cried bitter tears as I grieved for one of the finest friends I was ever to know. The joy I experienced a few months later and the Spiritual lift knew no bounds when I learned that he was alive and healthy.

There was no combat to fly, and with most of the oldtimers gone, time hung heavy with little to do. Jack Bradley began selecting ground officers from his old squadron to give them new assignments, and I started objecting that there were officers in my squadron too who should be considered for such jobs and promotions. Of course all the squadrons had good staff officers with long service, and each commander was naturally prejudiced in favor of his own men. I was a bit outspoken in my opinions to Jack, but he was no shrinking violet either, and made it clear that since he was the Group Commander he alone would make the decisions as to who would be assigned where. Jack was entirely right: in a combat zone assignments are made in the interests of the whole organization, and Jack was doing just that. I would have realized this for myself if I had given the matter much thought before shooting off my mouth, but personal loyalties sometimes blind one to the true issue. At any rate the minor disagreement was solved by my tending to my own business of running the 356th Squadron.

I was back with my old outfit for only a short time when I was called to IXXth Tactical Air Command to see General Weyland who asked me to go to Regensburg to assume command of the 405th Fighter Group. I was to prepare them for eventual shipment to the Far East for participation in combat against the Japanese. It was a pleasant surprise and challenge to receive the command of a fighter group, especially since combat was offered as a goal to work for.

I immediately asked Jack Bradley if he would release Major George M. Lamb for assignment in the 405th as Group Operations Officer in my new command. Jack was very cooperative, in agreeing that Lamb, a superior officer and pilot, would be of great value to me and in the bargain would stand a better chance for promotion.

I took over the 405th Fighter Group in the first week of June 1945, and Lamb and I hardly got our training program started when the unit was shipped to Camp Detroit near Laon, France, which was a holding camp for personnel being shipped to the Far East theater. While we were at Camp Detroit, however, the Japanese capitulated, and our plans for the Group were suspended. We were all happy and glad to see the end of the war; but it meant that now, instead of going to the Far East, the Group no doubt would be sent home for deactivation.

Lamb was very disappointed at the prospect of demobilization, because he had no wish to return to the States at this time and was seriously considering staying with the Air Corps as a career. He asked me if I thought he could return to the 354th Fighter Group which was scheduled for occupation duty in Europe. I was pretty sure we could arrange it, and I called Jack Bradley again, telling him of Lamb's problem. He was delighted to get Lamb back again; he requested Lamb's transfer, and I approved it. Reluctantly Lamb and I took leave of each other as he returned to our old outfit.

In October the call came to return to the United States, and we were sent by train to the Calais staging area at Marseilles. Our train accommodations, incidentally, were the famous "40 in 8" boxcars of World War I days, the cars being intended for "40 men or 8 horses." Within a short time the 405th, together with personnel from all branches of the Army, was loaded on a Liberty ship headed for Hampton Roads, Virginia, and as a Group Commander I was designated Troop Commander aboard ship for the journey home.

Arriving at Hampton Roads late one afternoon after approximately a week at sea, we debarked and were immediately entrained for the trip to Jefferson Barracks, Missouri. There I deactivated the group, after which all personnel were either discharged or released to inactive duty according to their individual status. I was offered a choice between accepting a regular commission or accepting the rank of lieutenant colonel in the reserves and reverting to inactive duty status. Wishing to return to college to complete my work toward a college degree, I accepted the reserve commission, and returned to my home.

CHAPTER 13

I spent two wonderful years after returning at Principia College. There I was privileged to meet and win the person who was to give substance and meaning to my life in the future. Patricia Ann Hayes and I were married following our graduation. My first job as the head of a household was as assistant football coach at the college. Following my coaching experience, I became established in Centralia, Illinois, as the manager of a prominent hatchery and settled down to what I thought would be many years of uninterrupted family bliss.

In the meantime I had been contacted by Jim Howard, who lived not far away in St. Louis, Missouri, and who now was a brigadier general in the Reserve. He wanted me to join his Active Reserve Unit, a Troop Carrier Wing based for training at Scott Air Force Base in Belleville, Illinois. Eager to work with and see Jim again I needed no second urging, and was given command of the Group eventually. As a fighter pilot I wasn't overly eager to get larger aircraft on my flight log record, but I soon learned to enjoy flying them. The big birds had tremendous stability under instrument conditions which was a pleasant change from the strict concentration and self-discipline required in the compact fighters to which I was accustomed. I spent much time flying with the Reserve from 1948 until the spring of 1951.

In 1951 it became more and more apparent to us in the Reserve that call up to active duty in the Korean conflict was imminent. It seemed logical that since I had been associated with cargo aircraft that I could now expect an active duty assignment involving them. To me as a fighter pilot, this was a fate worse than death. Word had it that we were destined to be sent to Travis Air Force Base in California for training as B-36 bomber pilots, and I began to get desperate. Jim Howard had already been sent to the general factory in the Pentagon, and I had no idea how to get in touch with him; I began to rack my brains for other contacts to whom I could appeal to escape the fate of becoming a bomber pilot. Somehow I got the word that Colonel George Bickell, my old CO of the 354th Fighter Group, was pulling duty at Eastern Air Defense Headquarters at Newburgh, New York, and I sent a wire to him revealing my predicament, and asking for help in getting back to a fighter assignment. In a short time the Reserve people at Scott AFB received a formal request from the Eastern Air Defense Force Deputy for Personnel—who turned out to be my old friend Colonel Jack Bradley—for my assignment to them because of my former fighter experience. It was a close squeak, but I was pulled off the bombing training list, and readied for shipment to EADF.

I was ordered to return to active duty on May 1, 1951, and directed to report to Otis AFB at Falmouth, Massachusetts for training in jet fighters. I proceeded to my new base where I started training in T-33s, and finished by flying F-86 Sabers. Transition to jets was a relatively simple matter in that they were so much more simple to operate, and the instincts and "feel" developed in piston engined aircraft applied equally to the heavier, smoother jets with a slight adjustment in application.

After completing my transition and becoming qualified in jets I was assigned to the 23rd Fighter-Interceptor Wing stationed at Presque Isle, Maine. Upon reporting to Colonel Charles H. MacDonald, Wing Commander, I was made first Operations Officer, and later Deputy Wing Commander. I worked with the 23rd until late in October. I was itching to get a chance to go to Korea to fly combat in the F-86, but I naturally assumed that I had little chance, for there were so many well-qualified pilots with uninterrupted service in the Wing who would rate first crack at any such opportunity. After all, I was just one of thousands of WW II retreads who could only boast of a few hours of jet experience. But intricate are the ways of fate and chance.

One day a request came from higher headquarters for the Wing to provide one field grade officer for ninety days temporary duty, purpose to accumulate jet combat experience by being attached for same to the 4th Fighter Wing stationed at Seoul, Korea. I took the request in to Colonel "Mac" and hinted that I was available and ready to leave; but as I had feared he was more practical about it. He sent word to our three squadron commanders that he had received the request for a volunteer for combat duty in Korea, and that he would decide from among their three requests which of them was to go. We waited for their requests to materialize, but oddly they never came.

I just bided my time, thinking if the eleventh hour arrived and still there were no volunteers, Mac would be forced to allow the poor old retread to fill the quota. My tactic worked perfectly. One squadron commander, it seems, had a wife about to deliver a baby, and he felt he should stay home. The second squadron commander revealed that he had been ill recently, and felt that he wasn't ready for combat just yet. The third squadron commander had decided to wait for the outcome of his application to the Command and Staff School. That left me the only field grade officer in the Wing stupid or healthy enough to volunteer for Korea. There was irony in this, for at the moment I was wearing a patch over my right eye due to an eye infection. But I wanted to go, and was designated the Wing volunteer.

With black patch and all, I, my wife Pat and the kids set off for Illinois where I would leave them with Pat's parents while I went to Korea to try my luck once again in combat. When we reached Bloomington, the inflammation in my eye flared up again, as I had run out of medication en route. They were able to take care of me at the local eye clinic, and gave me enough medication to get me through the trip to Korea.

I flew from Chicago to Travis AFB near San Francisco where I caught a MATS plane to Hawaii and Japan. I'll never forget the look on the officer's face when I reported in at FEAF Headquarters in Tokyo. He took one look at the patch over my eye, looked back at my orders, and said incredulously, "*You're* going to the 4th to fly combat in 86s? They must be hitting the bottom of the barrel back in the States if they're forced to send us one-eyed fighter pilots!" I assured him that I had two eyes, and that my right one was almost healed. Before catching a plane to Seoul I ran into an old WW II buddy who had been in the 356th Fighter Squadron with me, Major Earl Depner, who was now working in FEAF's Combat Operations Control. Having a chance to talk with an old friend before going to Korea helped in settling me down and squaring me away properly.

CHAPTER 14

I was flown to K-14 in Seoul where I reported to Colonel Harrison Thyng, the Wing Commander. He assigned me to the 335th Fighter Squadron for flight duty. The Squadron Commander, Major Winton "Bones" Marshall, welcomed me to the squadron, and when he found out that I had only minimun experience with F-86s, very considerately took extra time to fly with me and to check me out on formation and tactics. The first week I spent my time getting used to handling the F-86 under combat conditions. During this time I noticed I began to be annoyed by a very stiff and painful sensation in the back of my neck, which extended down the muscles across my shoulder blades. The condition persisted, and presented a real problem when I needed to turn my head for visual clearance sweeps. I reported to the Flight Surgeon who, lacking diagnostic equipment, finally made a calculated guess that the condition must have been caused by a cold that had settled into the muscle system. I was instructed to take a wintergreen oil rubdown and heat lamp treatment at the dispensary every morning after breakfast.

I soon began to participate in combat missions with the squadron, but was at a definite disadvantage, for the stiffness in my neck still prevented my getting good visual coverage. I found at first it was hard for me to find the MIGs. I couldn't understand why apparently everyone else could see them, and I couldn't. As it turned out, I was looking for them too close in. Now with jet speeds, they were about three times as far out as the Messerschmitts I had been used to spotting in Europe.

The F-86 responded to the slightest touch, and it could hold its own with anything, from the deck up to 25,000 feet. As I flew missions with the 4th, it was easy to divine their basic tactic. They flew up to the Yalu area at 45,000 feet, about 5000 feet below the lighter MIGs. (That was about as high as the F-86 could fly in formation with enough positive control to make it safe.) There they cruised around until they could entice the MIGs to make an attack, bringing them to the lower altitudes. The length of my temporary duty only allowed me to get in thirteen missions, and my lack of experience obliged me to fly wing on all but two missions.

On February 5, 1952, I flew my first flight lead on a morning mission to the Yalu area. We took off in pairs, pulling back to 94 percent climb out power, and turned right to climb out heading. A few minutes later we reached 45,000 feet in group formation, and headed for the Yalu where the squadrons took up separate patrol area patterns. A few minutes later we heard one of the other squadrons get bounced, and we dropped tanks and started searching for MIGs. About this time I saw an F-86 streak downward 500 yards ahead of me with a MIG hard after him. I dove to intercept the MIG with my 50-calibers firing way in front to distract him from the F-86. As I began to line-up behind the MIG, he broke off of his attack to the left. Starting to follow him, I heard my wingman calling for a break right, which I quickly executed. The MIG's wingman had been following him far enough behind so that I hadn't seen him, and was now queuing up on me. As I broke, the second MIG overshot me and plunged straight on down, depriving my wingman of a shot at him. The flight had stayed with me through all this, and we continued our searching for more MIGs. Oddly enough, we were unable to find a trace of any aircraft at all, friend or foe. The high jet speeds had scattered some eighty aircraft over a three- or four-hundred mile radius. The only evidence that a fight had taken place was an open parachute at about 25,000 feet which was slowly descending through the crisp cold air. The white and red chute stood out in brilliant contrast to the blue sky. Someone said over the RT, "That's a Gook chute," and we orbited the area until Bones Marshall called in, "Bingo," indicating he had hit 1500 pounds fuel remaining, the automatic go home count. Checking my own fuel, I found it hovering around 1500 pounds too, so I gave the hand signal to my flight, and we headed south for home.

In the Operations Shack I learned that some pilots thought that they had seen mirror flashes in the hills near Wonsan, just a hundred miles to the north of us on the east coast of the Korean Peninsula. They thought it might be a young lieutenant we had lost the day before in a forced bail out over that area. Bones Marshall had gotten permission from Combat Control to send a two-ship search flight to the area. He asked for two volunteers and since we were still in flight gear, my element leader and I asked to go.

We were determined to waste no time getting to the Wonsan area. We took off and climbed at full power. As we approached Wonsan a few minutes later, we let down to altitudes of less than a thousand feet for search patterns. We split up over the area and reduced power to normal cruise setting after pulling in the dive brakes. I was watching the ground intently for any telltale mirror flash or sign of any kind of the downed pilot as I hurriedly pushed the dive brake control button on top of the throttle forward. I should explain here that every American pilot carried with him a highly polished stainless steel mirror designed with a sighting hole in it, so that in the event of crash landing or bail out in enemy territory he could signal any friendly aircraft that happened to fly within range. Any pilot who saw such flashes from the ground took appropriate action to start rescue proceedings. If he had sufficient fuel he would stay and provide air cover until relieved. Lacking fuel, he would try to acknowledge the victim's signals by rocking his wings or rolling his craft, and then report the sighting to base over the radio. We didn't receive any ground fire as we made our search sweeps, and we concentrated on visual inspection of the ground below us fervently hoping to see some sign of life. We knew that the missing pilot had become engaged on his last rest and recreation trip to Japan, and we wanted to rescue him before word reached his fiancée that he was missing. We had been searching the ground below exhaustively for some 45 to 50 minutes, having covered around 400 square miles of the mountainous territory, but had seen no signs whatever to indicate that the reports had been valid.

As I pulled around to make a new sweep, I ran my eyes

over the instruments in an automatic check and was shocked to see that the fuel gauge registered 100 pounds. Estimating quickly, I guessed that I had enough fuel to go around the landing pattern maybe three or four times before landing without power, the only trouble being that I was over a hundred miles north of the landing field, and that one hundred miles was all enemy territory. I called my companion, asking for his fuel reading, and he replied that he had around 1800 pounds. I told him how low I was, and that I was heading for home plate. There was a moment's silence before the captain flying the other 86 acknowledged and said he would escort me back as far as I could make it. As I headed south in a climb, I automatically hit the dive brake flap control button forward, and the F-86 leaped as if released from a tether. The cause of my dilemma hit me like lightning. After let down I had somehow neglected to retract my dive brake flaps all the way flush with the fuselage. I had been cruising around with an imperceptible but deadly drag which had caused an excessive fuel consumption. No matter now; the fat was in the fire for certain, and I had some highly critical decisions to make. When we arrived over Wonsan we could see our Navy picket ships standing offshore in the distance. I could ditch near them in an emergency but the frigid ocean water of February didn't appeal to me at all, and I didn't even consider this solution as I climbed in the direction of Seoul.

I had two choices now: I could look for a place to crash-land as near as possible to the front lines, and try to sneak across to friendly troops; or I could climb as high as possible before flame-out and try to stretch my final glide in an effort to reach my own base. I couldn't accept the idea of landing the F-86 intact inside enemy territory, giving the North Koreans a perfectly good F-86 as well as a prisoner; so I decided to climb for altitude and give it a good try for home. As I climbed for altitude a bit of information gleaned from my past missions came to the surface of my mind. At 36,000 feet over Korea there was almost always a 100-knot prevailing wind from north to south. If I could reach it before final flame-out I could stretch my dead-stick glide to three or four times its normal length by riding this jet stream of air toward home.

As I reached 30,000 feet the reassuring throb of the J-47 jet engine died with heart-freezing abruptness. I knew that I still had about two or three minute's worth of fuel trapped behind the baffle plates in the fuselage fuel tank. The question was, did I want to restart and use the last drops to gain a precious 6000 feet of altitude toward the jet stream—or should I save the fuel for last-minute landing maneuvering. I decided that getting home was the paramount question, and I could worry about getting down later.

I nosed the fighter down to recapture the fuel, and ran through the air-restart procedure. That beautiful feel of surging power returned instantly as the engine came to life again, eagerly drawing the last of the free fuel from the tank. I again pointed the nose upward to extract the utmost altitude from my remaining power. I had to win that last 6000 feet. I passed 36,000 feet, and my hopes were just beginning to rise when the whine of the racing jet engine died with finality. I immediately pressed the stick forward, seeking the most efficient glide attitude. The captain flying beside me now urged me to try restarting once more, because he thought he could see fuel vapor trailing from my craft's tail pipe. I tried the restart procedure several times, but to no avail and I gave up, preferring to concentrate on navigating directly for base.

By now it looked as if we were almost three quarters of the way home, and I still had 15,000 feet of altitude. I began to review mentally the emergency dead-stick landing techniques recommended by test pilots of the F-86. The one that appealed to me and the one I hoped to use was a 270-degree three-quarter descending orbit from 10,000 feet over the downwind end of the landing runway. This one appealed to me, for I could make adjusting corrections all the way down by either widening my continuous turn into the runway or shortening it as needed. The one-time-only aspect of such a landing didn't escape me, for just several days before I had watched a Saber from the 53rd Group try one. The pilot had misjudged his approach, and went careening through the fighters and some B-26s parked on the other side of the field. He ended up being pulled from the pile of scrap metal he made out of his plane.

My tired spirits were restored now as I heard Tower Control calling me, confirming that traffic had been cleared for my emergency landing. I acknowledged their transmission, and told them I thought that I could make it. They replied with the cheering news that "the Meat Wagon and Fire Truck were standing by at mid-strip." "Thanks, a heap, *friend!*" I finished drily. I could see K-14 now, and began ever so gently to flatten my glide, hoping to reach the east end of the strip with at least 10,000 feet of precious altitude.

I made it! As the end of the strip slid under me far

below I dropped my gear and flaps, simultaneously dipping the nose to maintain flying speed of approximately 160 knots. If I made good my approach to the end of the runway I planned to pop my dive brakes at about one foot altitude which would stall me out and land the airplane in good shape with plenty of runway ahead. I was pretty careful now, for the accuracy of my judgment was a life and death matter from here in. I kept playing the turn to keep within gliding distance of the runway as I got lower and lower, and instinctively allowed my speed to build up over what I actually needed. Within limits excess speed could be gotten rid of safely, but only the Good Lord himself could provide it if you didn't have enough. I found myself crossing over the fence at 200 feet altitude and 200 knots, too much both ways, and if I didn't make corrections I knew I'd end up off the end of the runway with little pieces of F-86 wrapped around my gizzard.

I didn't know if this plane would side-slip or not with its swept wings, but I knew that with my old Mustangs in Europe this was a perfect way to kill speed and lose altitude in a hurry. Now I had the perfect opportunity to find out about the F-86 . . . Without hesitation I eased the stick forward and left, giving an offsetting right rudder adjustment at the same time. The F-86 dipped its left wing like a thoroughbred taking a gentle bit. It dropped gracefully, maintaining a good feel of control as the airspeed dropped smoothly and steadily. As the left wingtip came within five feet of the runway I had 120 knots on the clock, and as I leveled out over the middle of the runway she settled delicately to hover at about one foot over the runway at 110 knots. I popped the dive brakes, and she settled into the best landing that I ever believe I made.

All this took place in the first fifteen-hundred feet of the runway, and the F-86 rolled to the ramp intersection at mid-field where I had just enough speed left to turn off the runway and roll to a stop on the outer edge of the ramp area. As I slumped down in the cockpit, the first thought that flashed through my mind after the strained tension of the last twenty minutes was the title of Colonel Bob Scott's book, *God Is My Co-pilot.* I smiled in appreciation of the meaning of the phrase as I unbuckled to leave the cockpit.

I could see two or three jeeps racing out to meet me, and judging by the number of people crowded out on the flight lines, everybody on the base must have come out to watch me break my neck. Little did they know that the whole spectacle was caused by my own stupidity. The Wing Commander, Group Commander, and Squadron Commander pulled up in the jeeps, and all congratulated me on making it back, saving both my own skin and the aircraft. I thanked them, and rode back to Squadron Operations with the Squadron Commander with the sad recollection still in my mind that we had not found the missing pilot.

I flew a few more missions after my 100-mile glide from Wonsan, but my ninety days rapidly came to an end, and I prepared to return to the States and duty with the 23rd Wing at Presque Isle.

A day or so before I was due to leave the 4th Fighter Wing, I received word that Colonel Thyng would like to see me. I was at the dispensary getting one of my heat lamp treatments for my still-bothersome neck and back when the message reached me. Getting up from the soothing treatment I hurried to Colonel Thyng's quarters. After brief greetings, Colonel Thyng came right to the point, and asked me how I would like to take over command of the 4th Fighter Group. It came as a complete surprise to me. I knew the Group CO was due to be rotated back to the States, but I assumed they had someone already chosen to replace him.

I would give my eyeteeth for such a command, but nevertheless I hesitated. Although I had said nothing to the flight surgeon I knew that my injured back was, if anything, getting worse instead of better. I was having difficulty sleeping because of it, and I knew that the stiffness in my neck was influencing my performance as a pilot. I had never bothered to mention this because my tour of duty was nearly up, but this new development forced a decision right now. The Group was mine for the asking, and I was greatly tempted; but inside I knew that this was the wrong way, and that I owed more to the Air Force than my personal advancement at the possible cost of the interests of the Group.

I had made my decision! Regretfully I turned down the opportunity to command a fine Group, and it was a hard choice to make and stand by. Later my suspicions concerning the seriousness of my condition were borne out by the discovery that it was a return of my old injury in WW II when I had fallen from a fighter wing. The injury developed into arthritis of the spine, and this disability progressed to the point where the Air Force ultimately released me from active duty.

My disability is now rated as 100 percent, but I

wouldn't change a moment of my past experience in the Army Air Corps and the Air Force. Were the opportunity provided, I would eagerly do it all over again. No matter how the cost is calculated, my experience and associations were enriched in far greater measure. It is with great pride and gratitude that I recall the privilege of serving.

It is my fervent hope that neither my children, nor anyone's children, ever again need meet the extreme requirements of combat in defense of their country. But if that exigency should ever again present itself, it is my further hope and conviction that they, with an abiding reliance on their faith in God and in their heritage would arise to meet the need with the best effort of which they are capable. I can only hope and wish in that event that they would be fortunate enough to have as comrades-in-arms the same caliber of men with whom I was privileged to serve in my time.

356th Sqdn.

354th Ftr. Group, 9th Air Force

PILOT	CODE	a/c serial	TYPE	KILLS	A/C NAME
J.H. HOWARD	AJ-A	38374	P-51B	15	"DING HAO" 6 KILLS ETO 9 KILLS CBI w/AVG
R.E. TURNER	AJ-T	312434 415622	P-51B P-51D	12	"SHORT FUSE SALLEE"
R.E. GOODNIGHT	AJ-G	312213	P-51B	7¼	"MARY ANNE" DECEASED 1966 ELKO, NEVADA CORONARY
F.Q. O'CONNOR	AJ-O		P-51B	10½	"VERNA Q", "STINKY"
T.F. MILLER	AJ-M		P-51B	5½	"GNOMEE"
R.L. SHOUP	AJ-S		P-51B	5½	(MIA) "FER DE LANCE"
R.D. WELDEN	AJ-W		P-51B	5¼	"MACKIE"
G.M. LAMB	AJ-I		P-51B	7½	"UNO WHO", "NO FLIES"
H.E. FISK	AJ-F		P-51B	5	"DURATION PLUS"
B.G. TENORE	AJ-X	413581	P-51D	6	"THE PRODIGAL SON" MARCH AFB (DECEASED) A/C ACCIDENT
V.E. CHAMBERS	AJ-P		P-51B	3	"DEUCES WILD"
F.P. McINTYRE	AJ-M		P-51B	3	"SHANTY IRISHMAN" DECEASED A/C ACCIDENT
G.W. HALL	AJ-H		P-51B		"MISS L"
W.R. PERKINS	AJ-		P-51B		(KIA) HIT TREE STRAFING TRANSPORT ALONG FRENCH ROADS "CHOWHOUND"
M.A. GILLIS	AJ-		P-51B		"TEX"
L.E. JACKSON	AJ-J		P-51B		"STONEWALL"
R.J. KLOPOTEK	AJ-K		P-51B		"THE MAD POLE" (DECEASED) USA LIGHT A/C ACCIDENT
F. BORON	AJ-Q	463729	P-51D	4	"SNUFFY THE MAD POLE" INHERITED O'CONNOR'S A/C
E.F. BICKFORD	AJ-V	473137	P-51D	3½	"ALICE MARIE"
	AJ-U	463850	P-51D		"ELLES ANGEL"
	AJ-N	36358	P-51B		"CISCO"
F.Q. O'CONNOR	AJ-Q	226678	P-47D		"VERNA Q"
	AJ-U	312776	P-51B		
K.R. MARTIN				4½	GROUP CO FLEW WITH ALL SQDNS.
H.R. MITCHELL	AJ-		P-51B		"LIL HOMER PIGEON"
C.D. SHARMAN	AJ-		P-51B		"RED'N RUSTY"
E.G. DEPNER	AJ-D		P-51B		"BILLINGS BELL"
R.J. BROOKS	AJ-B		P-51B		

INDEX